THE ART OF LOVING GOD

The Art of Loving God

*Learning to Love and
Follow Jesus in Daily Life*

Rev. John H. Hampsch, C.M.F.

CHARIS

Servant Publications
Ann Arbor, Michigan

Charis Books is an imprint of Servant Publications designed especially to serve
Roman Catholics.

All Scripture, unless otherwise noted, has been taken from the HOLY BIBLE:
NEW INTERNATIONAL VERSION®, NIV®. Copyright 1973, 1978, 1984 by
International Bible Society. Used by permission of Zondervan Publishing House.
Selected texts have been taken from the Revised Standard Version of the Bible
(RSV).

The "NIV" and "New International Version" trademarks are registered in the
United States Patent and Trademark Office by International Bible Society.
Selected texts have also been taken from the following translations of the Bible,
copyrighted 1946, 1952, 1971 by the Division of Christian Education of the
National Council of Churches of Christ in the USA. Used by permission.

Published by Servant Publications
P.O. Box 8617
Ann Arbor, Michigan 48107

Cover design by Paul Higdon
Interior illustrations: *The Church Bulletin Clip Art Book* by Tom Finley, Regal
Books, Ventura, CA 93003. Used by permission.

96 97 98 99 10 9 8 7 6 5 4 3 2

Printed in the United States of America
ISBN 0-89283-913-9

Library of Congress Cataloging-in-Publication Data

Hampsch, John H.
    The art of loving God : learning to love and follow Jesus in daily
life / John H. Hampsch.
        p.   cm.
    ISBN 0-89283-913-9
    1. God—Worship and love.   2. Christian life.   I. Title.
BV4817.H36   1995
248.4—dc20   95-12663
                                                                   CIP

Contents

PREFACE

The Kiss of God

It was a cozy, chatty, pre-dinner cocktail conversation—just the newlyweds, with myself as the invited dinner guest in their living room. He was an open, warm, and ebullient person; she was gracious, but somewhat shy and reserved. Their mutual love was obvious, so my question-to-make-conversation was not out of place. "How did you two meet?" I queried.

"Would you believe it?" said Dave. "It was at an art auction, and we found ourselves bidding against each other. Of course, I won the bid," he smiled, "but I also won her as my wife. We dated for a year, but she wouldn't let me even kiss her until the wedding ceremony."

I opined that that was her retaliation for his having won the auction bid. We laughed together, as Janet blushed and started for the kitchen to serve the meal. But calling after her to make sure she heard, he teased, "But after I got the first kiss, the rest came easy!"

The young bride turned at the kitchen door long enough to cast a blushing smile at her chuckling spouse. Enough had been said for me to discern that this young man relished his victory; he had found the way to Janet's heart, though it took a year of self-control and patient love. But once he found how to reach her heart, it was forever open to him.

As I recalled that moment of light-hearted chitchat, it occurred to me that the same dynamic is found in God's design for us in pursuing our creature-Creator love relationship—the ultimate purpose of our very existence. It plays a part not only in the overall process of sanctification, but also in each step along the way to that goal of perfect union with God as we more and more abide in his love.

Each step of growth in holiness involves an attempt to encounter God in his love: we are drawn by the subtle magnetism of his grace, which "teases" us into a persevering pursuit. Eventually in a breakthrough of grace, the Lord kisses our soul with a tender touch of love before enticing us to the next step of the fascinating pursuit. The succinct exhortation of James says it all: "Come near to God and he will come near to you" (Jas 4:8). This dynamic is articulated more negatively—and facetiously—in a bumper-sticker sermonette: "If you feel far from God, guess who moved!"

Christians soon become aware that abiding in God's love must follow a Christic pattern: "Whoever claims to live in him must walk as Jesus did" (1 Jn 2:6). We must learn to "live a life of love, just as Christ loved us" (Eph 5:2). Only in this way will we "in all things grow up into him who is the Head, that is Christ" (Eph 4:15).

In retrospect, we might see that perhaps our first step began with a simple spirituality, epitomized by the unsophisticated ditty, "Jesus loves me, this I know, for the Bible tells me so."

With that foothold in kindergarten spirituality, we advance to the next stage where, "no longer infants" (Eph 4:14), we enjoy a more vigorous and athletic spirituality, "straining toward what is ahead" (Phil 3:13). At this stage, we also come to know and use the spiritual "supports" Our Lord gives us for the race.

In our third stage of growth, we come to appreciate the compassion and support of the "God of all comfort, who comforts us in all our troubles" (2 Cor 1:4). In the midst of the storms of life—the potholes, pitfalls, and panic—God guides us to a safe harbor, though he does not always calm the storm itself.

In our fourth stage, we find God's love spilling into our hearts with such abundance that it simply overflows to those around us, as we spontaneously become "devoted to one another in brotherly love, honoring one another" (Rom 12:10). This love, the fruit of the Spirit, spills forth in many forms from our hearts to all God's precious people. At this stage we come to experience in a profound degree what St. Augustine calls the primary characteristic of love, namely, "the liquefaction of the heart." That is, Spirit-melted hearts tend to "liquefy," spreading God's love to those around them. The "fluidity" of love makes it ever more penetrating into its environment.

In this unpretentious book, I have attempted to outline a four-part plan of action to lead you through each of these four stages in attaining union with God in love. Within each section, the individual chapters are certainly not meant to be an exhaustive list of techniques for attaining holiness. Rather, they are merely generically representative of countless possible approaches for fostering God's love in our souls, in response to his magnanimous love for each of us.

With all this in mind, let us take up our walking sticks and launch into the great adventure of a lifelong "walk with the Lord." For the person of good will, every step taken in sincerity will lead heavenward (see 1 Corinthians 15:58). Along the way, stop occasionally to relax contemplatively and enjoy the tender embrace and kiss of your divine companion—the God of love.

John H. Hampsch, C.M.F.

PART I

Back to Basics: Learning to Rely on a Loving God

One of nature's most fascinating learning processes takes place when an eaglet learns to fly. At the appropriate time, the mother eagle nudges the fledgling out of the lofty cliffside nest, and spirals around it as it falls fluttering toward the ground. Then she swoops under the little one, catches it on her back, and ferries it to a higher altitude before tipping it into another fall earthward, this time allowing it to fall closer to the ground before another last-minute rescue. With its wings strengthened by resisting the fall after each uplift, the eaglet eventually learns to fly.

Like eaglets, we experience a cycle of falls and rescues. Sometimes our loving Lord may appear to allow us to fall into weakness, apathy, fearful insecurities and even sin, before lifting us up to heights of holiness—only to let us plummet earthward again. Through this we are meant to learn the basic truth that in all of life's ups and downs, "God rescues and he saves" (Dn 6:27). In our moments of distress and plummeting discouragement, we may plead like the psalmist, "O Lord, how long will you look on? Rescue my life" (Ps 35:17). But as God's beloved faltering fledglings, we know that ultimately he will rescue us: "You are a shield around me, O Lord, you... lift up my head" (Ps 3:3). Eventually we recognize that we can count on his fathomless love for us—a reliable, trustworthy, accepting, magnanimous love that rescues, redeems, saves, and delivers us. "Turn, O Lord, and deliver me: save me *because of your unfailing love*" (Ps 6:4).

That is the first important lesson for us nestlings. Only when we have come to appreciate, in at least some of its many manifestations, that "unfailing love" as God's basic attribute can we respond to it and allow ourselves to be magnetized by it. Hence, in the chapters of this first section we shall consider a few of the manifold ways in which God patiently teaches us to rely on his awesome, wondrous unfailing love.

ONE

The Art of Loving God

*The parents of a five-year-old discovered
that their son was handicapped by poor sight,
so they arranged to have him fitted with eye-
glasses. But they were disturbed to find that he
always perched them on the end of his nose and
looked over the top of the lenses. "Why don't
you wear your glasses properly and look
through the lenses?" asked his father.*

*"Because," said the lad, "the glasses are so
nice and they help me see so much better that I
don't want to wear them out."*

We normally expect that the gifts we give others will be used
and appreciated. In the same way, God expects us to use appre-
ciatively the bounteous gifts he bestows on all of us. This is
especially true of God's greatest gift, the one about which
St. Augustine observed: "There's only one thing God doesn't
know. He doesn't know how he could give us a gift greater than
himself." But what exactly is this ultimate Gift, and what does it
mean to "use" it?

The beloved disciple offers a helpful, if somewhat enigmatic,
answer: "We know and rely on the love God has for us. God is
love. Whoever lives in love lives in God, and God in him"

(1 Jn 4:16). This suggests that "using" the Gift of God himself means simply "abiding in" or "living in" God's love.

Everyone who wishes to abide in God must first learn humility. Peter learned this healing lesson in an encounter with Jesus after the resurrection. Jesus adroitly showed the leader of the apostles that he hadn't been consistently abiding in love (and how can one "abide" without consistency?). As prophesied, Peter had experienced a triple love-failure during Jesus' trial, by his threefold denial before the cock-crow. It now boomeranged as a trial for Peter as he faced a triple questioning by the risen Jesus: *"Do you love me?"* (Jn 21:15-17). By eliciting a triple love-affirmation from Peter, Jesus tactfully provided a healing of his humiliating triple love-failure.

A closer look at this incident sheds some light on how humility can heal humiliation. We see that Jesus subtly engineered a threefold humbling for Peter. First, Jesus addressed Peter by his given name: Simon, son of John. This highlighted his humble origin and showed that he would be nothing without this very Jesus he had denied.

Second, although he had had a post-resurrection private encounter with Jesus (1 Cor 15:5), Peter still needed a public challenge in the presence of others. After all, he had pridefully set himself above those others: "Even if all fall away, I will not" (Mk 14:29). Fittingly, then, Jesus' first question to Peter was, *"Do you love me more than these do?"*

Last, Peter was humbled (verse 17 says "hurt") by having his love questioned not once but three times. For this newly exalted vicar of Christ, the lesson was painful but necessary. Love that is not humble is not true love.

HUMILITY—LOVE'S "TEST BY FIRE"

We too may need to linger over this first lesson in order to introject humility into our love. "Lord, I am ready to go with you to prison and to death" (Lk 22:33)—the apostle was chastened by his failure to live up to this boast. (We can only imagine what his thoughts must have been when he later heard Jesus prophesy his martyrdom—see Jn 21:19).

Like Peter, our claims of love of God may prove unfounded and even arrogant. We may like to think that our love would keep us faithful to God throughout the suffering of the end times that Jesus foretold: "In the time of punishment there will be great distress in the land and wrath against this people. They will fall by the sword and be taken as prisoners" (Lk 21:23-24). But could it be that our self-assurance of love and faithfulness is nothing more than arrogance? Is our faith-rooted love of God exceptional enough to face the coming trials of mankind's greatest disaster? "Because of the increase of wickedness, *the love of most will grow cold,*" Jesus warned (Mt 24:12). Will that "most" of mankind include us?

The only way to guard against this betrayal is to humbly follow Jesus' "rules of preparation" for his coming: "Be always on the watch, and *pray* that you may be able to escape all that is about to happen, and that you may be able to stand before the Son of Man" (Lk 21:36). "Lead us not into temptation," Jesus taught us to pray; or, as the *Jerusalem Bible* more correctly translates it, "Do not put us to the test" (Mt 6:13). And so, with each *fervent* "Our Father" our love becomes more humble and aware of God's protection.

Our love for God will not grow cold if we keep this protective power in mind, as so many of the psalms encourage us to do. "Spread your protection over those who love your name" (Ps 5:11). "The Lord watches over all who love him, but all the wicked he will destroy" (Ps 145:20). "'Because he loves me,' says the Lord, 'I will rescue him; I will protect him... I will answer him; I will be with him in trouble; I will deliver him and honor him'" (Ps 91:14-15).

LOVE IS A MANY-SPLENDORED THING

Some background information will help us to better understand the poignant dialogue we have been examining, from

John 21. "Do you love me?" Jesus asks. "You know that I love you," Peter answers. But each is using a different word for "love," and each word has very different connotations.

In Greek, the language of the New Testament, there are several words for love. *Philia* was a common word that signified a tender, warm, "feeling" kind of love that is perhaps best described as brotherly love, or the affection of close friendship. Prior to Jesus' teachings on love, *philia* was the most sublime form of human love known. It was a deep love—deep enough to entail willingness to die for a friend.

But the love that Jesus taught (using his native tongue, Aramaic) was qualified with characteristics that transcended even the beautiful *philia* kind of love. So the early Scripture writers adopted another Greek word for love—*agape*—for use in the New Testament, and they enriched it with more sublime connotations than it had enjoyed in secular speech and writings. *Agape* came to describe God's kind of love—a God "who so *loved* the world that he gave his one and only Son" (Jn 3:16). It entails even more than willingness to die for a friend: it entails willingness to die for an enemy. It is a generous, sacrificial, Christlike love that Paul describes as a "willingness to die for the powerless, for the ungodly, for sinners and for those at enmity with God" (Rom 5:6-10).

Peter and the other disciples did not know about the *agape* kind of love at the time of their post-resurrection encounter with Jesus. Why? Because *agape* love is a fruit of the Spirit (Gal 5:22) and is God's own love "poured out into our hearts by the Holy Spirit" (Rom 5:5); it required a pentecostal outpouring of that Spirit, which "had not yet been given" (Jn 7:39).

This explains why John's Gospel, which was written in Greek, employs both these words to translate "love." Jesus uses *agape* in his first two questions, but Peter replies using *philia* all three times. Twice Jesus asks, "Do you love [*agape*] me?" And Peter answers, "Yes, you know that I love [*philia*] you." The third time he asks the question, Jesus substitutes the word *philia*—as if to say, "Do you love me even with a lesser [*philia*] love?" Jesus understood the process of spiritual maturation, and knew that in time Peter would indeed come to love him more and more.

This should not encourage us to indulge in an immature, "God loves me the way I am" mentality. Instead we must listen for God's response to our faltering steps of faith: "I love you too much to *leave* you the way you are!"

Can any of us say that we *really* obey God's most basic command? "Love the Lord your God with all your heart and with all your soul and with all your strength.... These commandments are to be upon your hearts. Impress them on your children. Talk about them when you sit at home and when you walk along the road, when you lie down and when you get up" (Dt 6:5-7). This is no mere counsel. Jesus affirmed that the command to love God is the first and greatest mandate for human creatures (Mt 22:38). We will never fully attain total and perfect love, of course. But if we think of ourselves as already "good enough," we sabotage our very striving toward the goal.

How do we know if we're really striving to reach that norm? God's holy Word answers that question clearly, frequently, firmly and unevasively. John says, "This is love for God: to obey his commands" (1 Jn 5:3). Also with emphasis, Jesus puts it another way: "Not everyone who says to me, 'Lord, Lord' will enter the kingdom of heaven, but only he who *does the will of my Father*" (Mt 7:21). Love of God is not "a warm fuzzy"—although for some mystic souls it may entail a depth of emotion that reaches even beyond ecstasy. Essentially, our love for God is an uncompromising obedience to his will and laws.

God's will is revealed in the *divine* laws handed down by his Church (laws against euthanasia, abortion, and birth control fall into this category), but also in the divinely backed *human* laws officially established by that same Church (canon laws regarding priestly celibacy, for example, or church precepts regulating fasting, Mass attendance, confession, and Communion). The scriptural basis for love-authenticating obedience to such laws is extensive. Jesus says, "He who listens to you listens to me; he who rejects you rejects me" (Lk 10:16). And again, "Whatever you bind on earth will be bound in heaven, and whatever you loose on earth will be loosed in heaven" (Mt 16:19; see also Matthew 18:18). Paul demands obedience to church authority (see 1 Thessalonians 5:12; 1 Timothy 5:17; Hebrews 13:7). A detailed examination of conscience in these matters will reveal clearly just how much we *really* love God.

Of course, Jesus as the God-man is our contact point with God: "No one comes to the Father except through me" (Jn 14:6). When Jesus asked Peter, "Do you love *me?*" he was inquiring about the apostle's love for God. And when we obey the mandates of Jesus, we obey the mandates of the Father, in the Spirit: "If anyone loves me, he will obey my teaching. My Father will love him, and we will come to him and make our home with him. He who does not love me will not obey my teaching.... The Spirit whom the Father will send will teach you and remind you of everything I have said" (Jn 14:23-26). Paul encouraged the Thessalonians to persevere in such love-authenticating obedience to God and to Christ: "We have confidence that you will continue to do the things we command directing your hearts into God's love and Christ's perseverance" (2 Thes 3:4-5). Likewise, our *obedience*—Christ-centered and thus God-centered—will be a sign that our love for God is deep and persevering.

THE POWER OF ONE ACT OF LOVE

What is the greatest single act a human can perform? Saints and theologians tell us that an act of love of God is the greatest and most perfect action anyone could ever aspire to, either in heaven or on earth. A single act of *agape* love immediately restores or deepens the soul's mysterious union with God (see John 14:23). Even someone who is in mortal sin can return to a state of grace and baptismal innocence by a single sincere act of love of God. (By church law, however, Catholics must later confess any mortal sin to a priest before receiving Communion, even though grace is restored immediately.) A single act of love of God can dissolve venial sin and imperfections on the soul, can lessen accumulated purgatorial suffering and restore lost merits. It has an intercessory power to elicit God's grace for the conversion of sinners, sometimes by a deathbed repentance; it can help the souls in purgatory; it can bring divine comfort to the afflicted and can draw down from heaven special graces for the clergy, to fill them with strength, light, and zeal.

St. John of the Cross tells us that the smallest act of perfect love of God is more effective and meritorious than all other conceivable good works put together. Some theologians regard these *perfect* acts of love as very difficult to perform: they require *total* detachment from sin and habits of sin, along with sincere desire for union with God as the most desirable of goals. But even if our love falls short, one relatively feeble act of love— a simple, heartfelt prayer such as, "My God, you are good. I truly love you!"—can still release enormous power and gain fathomless graces.

Such acts of love of God can be made silently or aloud wherever we may be—in a crowd, alone in bed, while waiting for a stoplight or an elevator or a waitress, or during a TV commercial. Some people may find it easier to express their love while gazing on a devotional picture of the Sacred Heart of Jesus or on a colorful sunset. Others may be stirred to acts of love while holding a child or fondling a pet—or even while luxuriating in a warm shower, with loving thankfulness to a God who provides such amenities. Whatever the setting, God is ever present, listening and waiting with breathless yearning for a tiny burst of love from a precious soul that acknowledges him for his fathomless goodness.

Love is a virtue technically called charity. And a virtue is technically a spiritual habit. Now, any habit can be strengthened by frequent and more intense repetition. As St. Thomas Aquinas reminds us, "One learns to walk by walking; one learns to talk by talking; and one learns to love by loving." Through constant practice, our habit of love will become more and more deeply rooted and we will be able to answer Jesus' query, "Do you love me?" with a volley of acts of *agape* love. Thus we will follow Paul's prayerful exhortation: "May your love abound more and more" (Phil 1:9).

Paul was someone who had insight into the God-designed reward awaiting those who have mastered the art of loving God. But how can anyone describe the indescribable? Paul simply rephrased the words of Isaiah 64:4: *"No eye has seen, no ear has heard, no mind has conceived what God has prepared for those who love him"* (1 Cor 2:9).

TWO

SECRET

The World's Greatest Secret

> *"Besides me, have you told anyone else about your secret marriage?"* a lady asked her friend.
>
> *"No,"* replied the other, *"I'm waiting for my husband to sober up. After you, I want him to be the first to know."*

We Christians are privy to the world's greatest secret—a "secret that for ages past was kept hidden in God" (Eph 3:9). Paul tells the Colossians that "this secret which has been kept hidden for ages and generations is now disclosed to the saints [believers]" (Col 1:26), but he reminds the Romans that it was veiled in prophecies of ages past (see Romans 1:2; 16:26). To the Corinthians he describes it as a "secret *wisdom*—a wisdom that God destined for our glory before time began and has now revealed to us by his Spirit" (1 Cor 2:7-10).

Peter remarks that even prophets and angels longed to fathom the secret things of God but were not given this privilege (see 1 Peter 1:10-12). And Jesus himself also highlights the same point—that this privileged information has now been revealed to us: "Many prophets and kings wanted to hear what you hear and did not hear it" (Lk 10:24).

But what, precisely, is this great secret of which Paul exults in being the emissary (see Ephesians 3:9)? He summarizes it in three words: *"Christ in you"* (Col 1:27). Simple words, but so pregnant with meaning that it will take us all eternity to fathom their spiritual significance! Perhaps this is why Paul adds a descriptive phrase as sort of epilogue to his three-word secret: "the hope of glory."

In view of the awesome privilege that is ours in being privy to this now-revealed secret, a somewhat disturbing question arises: Are we "sober" enough—that is, spiritually sensitive enough—to be impacted by this simple yet profound reality? The question itself is sobering.

Jesus said that the world at large lacks this required spiritual sensitivity, "neither seeing nor knowing" (Jn 14:17). All three synoptic gospels show him quoting Isaiah about those who are "ever hearing, but never understanding... ever seeing, but never perceiving" (Is 6:9; see also Matthew 13:13, Mark 4:12, Luke 8:10).

But although the riches of Christ are unsearchable, Paul assures us that for those who have eyes to see, this manifold wisdom can be known *through the Church*. Not only that, Paul explains in the same passage: part of the mystery consists in the fact that even the great spiritual powers in the heavenly realms can attain this insight only through the Church on earth (see Ephesians 3:8-10). Isn't it staggering? The Church is a mirror through which angelic entities see the glory of God—besides what they see directly in the beatific vision of heaven itself. That's why Peter says, "Angels long to look into these things" (1 Pt 1:12). The spiritual maturity of church members on earth—of you and me—will determine how the wisdom of God is portrayed to these heavenly powers. No wonder Paul goes on to urge us to "live a life worthy of the calling you have received" (Eph 4:1)!

Of course, only spiritually mature souls are given deep insight into this secret of "Christ in us." "The Lord takes the upright into his confidence" (Prv 3:32). "He confides in those who fear him; he makes his covenant known to them" (Ps 25:14). To such people "he reveals deep and hidden things" (Dn 2:22, 28).

To really *know* the Christ in us, we must first have the Spirit of Christ in us. On this subject, Paul uses strong words: "If anyone does not have the Spirit of Christ in him, he does not belong to Christ" (Rom 8:9). Also, we must always be ready to obey God's will. "Lord, why do you intend to show yourself to us and not to the world?" Jude asked at the Last Supper (Jn 14:22). Jesus replied that *loving obedience* to his will (his teachings) would make the difference. This is what Moses had received and handed on as the norm for grasping God's secret revelation: "The secret things revealed belong to those who *obey all the words of his law*" (Dt 29:29).

Most Christians "know" the simple fact that Christ abides in them. For many, though, it is only a theological or catechetical type of knowing, a cerebral knowledge that remains merely academic. But this truth calls for a deep, experiential type of knowing—a heart knowledge which is a life-changing, transforming, truly privileged insight. Scripture refers to this insight so often—for example, in Paul's famous prayer:

> I pray that... through his Spirit... Christ may dwell in your hearts through faith. And I pray that you, being rooted... in love, may have power... to grasp how wide and long and high and deep is the love of Christ, and to know [experience] this love that *surpasses knowledge*—that you may be filled to the measure of all the *fullness* of God.
>
> **Ephesians 3:14-19**

"All the fullness of God"—what superlatives this phrase expresses! How can mere mortals grasp such a concept? It would be like trying to drink the oceans dry. No wonder heaven has to be eternal; we cannot exhaust the infinitude of God. Yet, amazingly, we partake of this abundance: "of his *fullness* we have all received one blessing after another" (Jn 1:16). But there is more. Since the "*fullness* of God dwells in Christ" (Col 1:19; 2:9), then it can be said that with Christ in us, our humanity becomes a tabernacle for God's divinity. Paul wanted Christ to be "exalted" in his body, adding with profound mystical insight, "For me, to live is Christ" (Phil 1:21). In some mysterious way, we too are called to become "incarnational" or "Christlike" in every aspect of our lives. How deeply we perceive this mystery or secret will be proportionate to how closely we replicate the holiness of the divine Lord within us.

TESTS OF SPIRITUAL MATURITY

Our growth into the spiritual maturity that brings insight into this great secret of "Christ in me" is a gradual process. How can we gauge our progress? Let me suggest a few criteria.

1. **Is my grasping for an "it" becoming an embrace of a "him"?** As we mature, we strive less for particular virtues, fruits of the Spirit, or charismatic gifts, and focus instead on their *source*—Jesus himself. We remain aware of these beautiful expressions of God's love, but we are occupied with the God of love himself. Children are fascinated with their Christmas gifts; adults appreciate the givers more than the gifts. On a spiritual level too, our appreciation becomes more person-oriented than thing-oriented as we mature.

2. **Am I becoming more aware that the Person I perceive as the Christ within me is triune?** "God the Father of all . . . is in all," says Paul (Eph 4:6); "God the Son, Jesus Christ is in you" (2 Cor 13:5); and "God the Holy Spirit is in you" (1 Cor 6:19). Perhaps we think of God in a way that St. Thomas Aquinas calls "attribution": we attribute to one Person of the Trinity a work that belongs to all three—to the Father, creation; to the Son, redemption; to the Holy Spirit, sanctification. Naturally, because Jesus took on the same human nature we have, we relate most easily to him. He is our access to the Deity (Jn 14:6, 11). But as we become

more spiritually mature, this human character of Jesus will open us to the transforming influence of all three Persons. Thus, we will gain more profound insight into the three personalities of the one God within us.

3. Am I learning that holiness is more a side effect than a goal? Certainly, God wills that all should become holy (1 Thes 4:3). But as we mature spiritually, we see that holiness results from the presence and work of Christ in us. We must learn to concentrate on immersing our life in Christ and leaving the outcome to God working in us by his grace. Seeking holiness on our own without this focus is like trying to get a suntan by striking matches in a dark room. Get out and bask in the brilliant sunlight!

4. Do I value God's approval most of all? As we mature spiritually, we seek God's approval for all we do. And we enjoy it far more than we enjoy the plaudits of any humans who may admire our spiritual accomplishments and be edified by them. "How can you believe," Jesus asks, "if you accept praise from one another, yet make no effort to obtain the praise that comes from the only God?" (Jn 5:44).

5. Is Scripture helping me to know Jesus better? Love of Scripture is certainly a worthy goal (2 Tm 3:15), yet in those who are less mature it may lean toward a "bibliolatry," as if it were an end in itself rather than a telescope for exploring the mystery of Jesus. "You diligently search the Scriptures because you think that by them you possess eternal life," Jesus warned some of the religious leaders who opposed him. "But these are the Scriptures that testify about *me*, yet you refuse to come to *me* to have life." (Jn 5:39-40). As we grow in maturity, we will not fall into this same mistake.

6. Am I depending less and less on myself and more and more on Jesus, in ways that pervade every aspect of my

life? Becoming mature means recognizing that our faith is not mountain-moving by itself but that it becomes so once it is fused with Jesus' faith before the Father. Then we truly understand the words of Jesus: "Without me you can do nothing" (Jn 15:5). And with Paul, we become convinced that "this all-surpassing power is from God, not us" (2 Cor 4:7).

The Spirit of Jesus is all that our spirit needs to accomplish wonders. His heart beats with the love that our heart needs; his ministry has the effectiveness that our ministry needs. As we grow in surrender to him, the meaning of the great "secret" unfolds more and more. His abundant life is released to sweep away disease and sin; his life-giving water floods us with his vigor for living.

7. **Do Christlike patterns of behavior show more clearly in my life?** The fruit of the Spirit that characterizes maturing Christians reflects *Christlike* behavior patterns, not just new ones. Jesus did not say "abide in love," but "in *my* love"; he did not say "I give you joy," but "I give you *my* joy"; he did not say "peace I give you," but "*my* peace I give you." The maturing soul becomes conformed to Christ by the Holy Spirit in every phase of living.

8. **Is Christ's presence becoming more and more of a reality in me?** As we offer our bodies, minds, and wills to God, we become living testimonies of Jesus alive in the world today. Just as Jesus elicited a subtle sense of wonder from those he encountered (see John 7:15, for example), so will we—to the extent that people can sense the living presence of Jesus in us.

9. **Would I describe my awareness of Christ in me as sporadic or continuous?** Those who are spiritually mature are deeply aware of Christ's inner presence—like Mary whose soul *magnified* the Lord (see Luke 1:46). Sometimes this awareness is a backdrop to the frenetic activities of daily life;

often it moves to the foreground in an experience of mystical contemplation. Whatever the case, spiritual maturity brings greater insight into God's wondrous work in us: "And we, who with unveiled faces all reflect the Lord's glory, are being *transformed into his likeness* with ever-increasing glory, which comes from the Lord, who is the Spirit" (2 Cor 3:18).

This nine-point test might provide a framework for Paul's mandate: "Examine yourselves to see whether you are in the faith; test yourselves. Do you not *realize* that Christ is in you—unless of course you fail the test?" (2 Cor 13:5).

What a privilege to have discovered this great secret! Let us explore it beginning today, for this is the most important and exciting pursuit we could ever hope for. As Paul reminds us, "God has chosen to *make known* the glorious riches of this mystery, *CHRIST IN YOU....* we proclaim him, admonishing and teaching with all wisdom, so that we may present everyone perfect in Christ" (Col 1:27-28).

THREE

Four Types of Counterfeit Faith

The hand-written note taped to the button panel of a hotel elevator read: "Button for floor eight is out of order; press three and five instead." Amused, I watched a young couple trying to reach the eighth floor fall for the hoax. Suppressing my laughter, I left the bewildered couple in the elevator as I exited on the tenth floor.

There are many things in life besides elevator buttons for which there is no adequate substitute. One of them is authentic faith—the charismatic gift of faith that assures us our prayers will be answered. This God-given and God-focused certitude admits of no substitutes. Surrogate forms of faith may render our prayer petitions ineffectual.

The *virtue* of faith—as distinguished from the charismatic gift of faith—is primarily the belief in God as revealer of truth (by the Spirit through Jesus); secondarily, it is the belief in those very truths, or doctrines, he has revealed. Believing that our prayers will be answered is not the virtue of faith, but the gift of faith.

This gift of faith is a help from God, but we must guard and cultivate it. Unfortunately, many people are deceived and misdirected in matters concerning faith. Here are a few of the forms in which counterfeit faith is usually disguised:

1. **Faith in one's faith.** This is perhaps the most subtle form of ersatz faith. It is wrongly directed, since it focuses on oneself more than on God. It often manifests itself as "claiming" faith, putting into action what Jesus says in Mark 11:24: "Therefore I tell you, whatever you ask for in prayer, believe that you have received it, and it will be yours." But it is important to read this passage in context, for it makes no mention of a God-focus and can be wrongly interpreted with a humanist slant. The truth of its message emerges only when the verse is taken in conjunction with a previous one: "Have faith *in God*"—or, as one translation has it, "Have the faith *of God*" (Mk 11:22).

   "Faith in one's faith" is also the most prideful form of counterfeit faith. It is most often found in people who pride themselves on their great faith. (I'm tempted to ask such persons how many mountains they've moved lately!)These are frequently the same individuals who wrongly think that by "exerting" their faith their prayers will be answered; they grit their teeth (at least symbolically), striving to believe that their requests will be granted. With all this straining—often accompanied by a sense of being overwhelmed by the problems at hand—it is easy to lose sight of the problem-solver, Jesus.

   While Peter had enough faith to walk on water, he began to sink when he shifted his focus from Christ to the threatening waves (see Matthew 14:30). His faith was defective and Jesus rebuked him for it, calling him a man of "little faith." Peter refocused on Christ with his cry of panic, "Lord, save me"— which is what we must learn to do. Our faith must be faith in God, not faith in our faith, no matter how pressured we may feel.

2. **Faith in one's prayer.** This counterfeit form of faith does not look primarily to God for its power either. It focuses on

the prayer itself, rather than leaning on the Lord for help. It is somewhat impersonal and does not reflect confidence in God. When we exercise this type of "faith," our prayer loses its calm expectancy and trust in God; it becomes intense and acquires an aura of urgency and anxiety. We forget the Lord's fatherly kindness and his desire to provide for our needs: "If you... know how to give good gifts to your children, how much more will your Father in heaven give... to [his children] who ask him?" (Lk 11:13).

Since this form of counterfeit faith tends to be demanding rather than trusting, those who wish to move on in the Lord must make a sort of leap of faith. Like trapeze artists, we have to let go and *trust* that strong arms will catch us after our dizzying, mid-air somersaults of confusion and questioning, trials and pain. Paul encourages us to exercise this true faith. "*Do not be anxious about anything,*" he says, "but in everything, by prayer and petition, with thanksgiving, present your requests to God" (Phil 4:6).

Anxiety-free prayer thanks God even *before* the answer comes! Jesus exemplified this in his own prayer: "Father, I thank you that you have heard me. I know that you always hear me, but I said this for the benefit of the people... that they may believe" (Jn 11:41-42). Let this be for us a model of the true faith that puts its trust, not in prayer itself, but in the God who answers prayer.

3. **Faith in a human as God's instrument.** This form of counterfeit faith, like the two above, also lacks proper God-focus. We see it in certain types of healing services, for example, where attention is focused on human "faith-healers" rather than on the Lord.

Clearly, God gives gifts such as healing to some persons far more abundantly than to others (see 1 Corinthians 12), and some become developed and refined to the point where they are not just gifts but recognized ministries. Sometimes these are so amazing that it is difficult not to focus our faith on the human agent. But we must remember the source, placing our faith in *God* who gives every good gift (Jas 1:17) and empowers his servants. "In me... he will bear much fruit; apart from me you can do *nothing*" (Jn 15: 5).

Many healing evangelists and other spiritually gifted persons do humbly give all the glory to God. The problem lies with some of the persons who are healed through their gifts. In theory they acquiesce to the truth, but in practice they praise the human healers without giving glory *exclusively* to God whose instruments these are. This dilutes their faith and often impedes the work of healing (as it also does with other spiritual gifts such as prophecy and words of knowledge). The psalmist expresses the opposite of this counterfeit faith that centers on the human agent: "I will come and proclaim your mighty acts, O Sovereign Lord; I will proclaim your righteousness, yours alone" (Ps 71:16).

4. Posterior faith without prior faith. "Prior faith" causes miracles, while "posterior faith" is caused by them. *Posterior* faith is activated or stimulated by witnessing a healing or miracle. It is an exercise of the *virtue* of faith that makes us believe more in God's goodness, omnipotence, or love.

Prior faith, on the other hand, is faith that causes or induces God's remarkable intervention. Unlike posterior faith, prior faith is not a virtue but a mountain-moving charismatic *gift* (see 1 Corinthians 12:9; 13:2). Both prior and posterior faith are good, of course, and neither is counterfeit in itself. But Jesus clearly teaches that prior faith is of a higher caliber than posterior faith: "Because you have seen you have believed; blessed are those who have not seen and yet have believed" (Jn 20:29). To the extent that we lack this more perfect prior faith, which is essential to our spiritual life, then we can be said to have counterfeit faith. If we do not fulfill the Lord's expectations in this regard, then we are *less authentically* Christian than we are called to be.

It is clear that Jesus expects us all to be faith-filled miracle-

workers, not just faith-excited miracle-*observers.* "Whatever you ask for in prayer, believe that you have received it, and it will be yours" (Mk 11:24). "I will do whatever you ask in my name" (Jn 14:13). "Ask and it will be given you" (Mt 7:7). This prior faith is required not just when asking for favors or miracles from God but also for performing miracles oneself.

As with the apostles, our growth may start with the less-perfect posterior faith. This is what they experienced after seeing the water-to-wine miracle at Cana, where Jesus "revealed his glory and his disciples [then] put their faith in him" (Jn 2:11). But Jesus called the apostles to the more sublime form of faith that *produces* miracles: "I tell you the truth, anyone who has faith in me will *do* what I have been doing. He will *do* even greater things than these" (Jn 14:12). The Gospels show Jesus charging the apostles to exercise this prior faith (see Matthew 10:1-10, for example); the Acts of the Apostles shows their response.

What kind of people does Jesus expect to be miracle-workers, not just miracle-observers? "Anyone who has faith in me"—namely, everyone who is called Christian. And so we must grow into faith that is authentically Christian—that flourishes because of miracles and that also causes miracles to flourish. Anything less is defective Christian faith.

Just as there are ways of testing counterfeit currency, so also there are ways of testing counterfeit faith. I hope that this attempt to outline four of its most blatant forms will help you grow in the authentic faith to which Jesus is calling you.

FOUR

Treatment for Anemic Christians

A baby snake asked its mother, "Are we poisonous, Mommy?"
"Yes," she responded. "Why do you ask?"
"Because I just bit my tongue!" he wailed.

We all have elements of self-destruction within us. Paul recognized this internal poison or "fruit for death" (Rom 7:5) as the "sin living in me" (7:17). Yet he rejoiced that its antidote is available "for those who are in Christ Jesus" (8:1).

Knowing that Jesus is our antidote for sin and failure is a critical aspect of Christian spirituality. If we neglect it, we will soon grow spiritually anemic and weakened by sin. Why, then, do we lose this critical focus? Most often because we tend to seek immunity from evil in some*thing*, rather than some*one*. We refer to receiving "salvation" or "grace" or a "blessing"—and of course all of these have true meaning for a Christian. Yet none is the real antidote. Overarching such spiritual benefits is the ultimate, indescribable gift—a *Person*, not a thing; God's own Son, "he *himself* who bore our sins... so that we might live for righteousness" (1 Pt 2:24). Jesus himself—and he alone—is our antidote.

All this seems obvious, doesn't it? We know that salvation requires a savior, grace a bestower, blessings a blesser. Yet the fact remains that we tend to seek gifts more than the giver; we look for answers to our prayers more than we seek the one who answers them; we focus more on our problems than on the problem-solver. The disciples did this too. When Jesus was walking on the water toward them, they were terrified and needed a reminder to focus on Jesus—not on their fear, not on a "ghost": "It is *I*. Don't be afraid" (Mt 14:27).

Likewise, we need to center our attention on Jesus. Without this critical focus, we will meet with futility and frustration as we search for antidotes to the inner poison of our sinfulness, our weaknesses, and our repeated failures. In this section we will examine some of the areas in which a Christ-focus is essential; but first let us look at a few of the patterns of failure through which this focus can be lost.

FAILURE BY APATHY

Sometimes our response to a time of grace is not a no, but neither is it enthusiastic. Such was the case of King Jehoash, who was directed by the prophet Elisha to strike the ground with his arrows. This he did, but only three times. "You should have struck the ground five or six times," the angry prophet cried out; "then you would have defeated Aram and completely destroyed it" (2 Kgs 13:19). As a result of his half-hearted response, Jehoash defeated the Arameans only three times, instead of achieving total victory.

Another story illustrates the opposite type of response. A newly appointed prison chaplain noticed two chairs draped in black near the chapel pulpit. He was told they were reserved for two men who were to be executed after the Sunday service he was preparing. His sermon would be the last they would ever hear. Imagine how conscientiously the chaplain prepared that sermon! Imagine also how attentively those death-row inmates absorbed the words of the preacher!

There are indeed special moments of grace which stir us to apply ourselves intensely. Most often, however, our spiritual response is more cavalier than enthusiastic. But, as some quipster has put it, the sobering truth is that "what we go after here determines where we go hereafter."

FAILURE BY PROCRASTINATION

There was a strategy meeting in hell, the story goes, and Satan asked his demons to brainstorm about how to accelerate the ruination of souls on earth. One demon suggested tempting people to believe there is no heaven. That idea was rejected because everyone knows that good must have its reward. A second demon suggested tempting people to believe there is no hell. That too was rejected because everyone who experiences guilt expects punishment. A third demon suggested that humans be tempted to believe that there is no hurry. This would allow fleeting graces to pass unused; inspirations would not be acted upon, and souls would thus wither spiritually and be easily seduced. Of course, this strategy was unanimously accepted. Today it is one of the most formidable in the devil's armamentarium.

Our response to the urgings of grace must be timely—that is, we must act within the optimum time frame that is often delineated by a special providence of God. "As long as it is day we must do the work of him who sent me," said Jesus. "Night is coming when no man can work" (Jn 9:4).

Delay, or procrastination, is the archenemy of grace. It aborts the flow of grace through all kinds of distractions: worldly entanglements—"I have just bought a field, and I must go see it" (Lk 14:18); family affairs—"Let me first bid farewell to my family" (Lk 9:61); suspended belief—"We'll hear you later about this," as the Athenians told Paul (Acts 17:32); personal convenience—"When I find it convenient, I will send for you," said Governor Felix, to sidestep Paul's witnessing (Acts 24:25).

A boy missed his bus and started running after it but finally gave up. A passerby asked, "What's the matter, son? Couldn't you run fast enough?"

"Oh yes," the boy replied. "I just didn't start soon enough!"

If we procrastinate we too will be left behind in the dust. Grace delayed is grace lost.

FAILURE BY REFUSAL

More common than failure due to apathy or procrastination is failure through saying an outright "no" to the promptings of divine grace. The following little poem, titled "But I Didn't," is a kind of examination of conscience for this type of failure:

Did you ever think at the close of day
Of kindly words you meant to say—but didn't?
Do you ever think when day is done
Of errands you kindly could have run—but didn't?
Do you ever think when skies are red
Of hungry mouths you could have fed—but didn't?
Do you ever think at dawn or night
Of letters that you meant to write—but didn't?
Will you think at life's last setting sun
Of all the deeds you could have done—but didn't?

Anonymous

CHRIST-FOCUS IN THE EUCHARIST

These self-destructive patterns of failure can distort our spiritual vision in countless ways by subtly depersonalizing our relationship with Jesus. How can this out-of-focus Christianity distance us from Christ? There are many possibilities.

Consider, for instance, how it has caused many to regard the Eucharist as a mere symbol, rather than the living person of Jesus with whom we are fused in Communion. Ponder carefully and prayerfully Jesus' emphatic teaching at Capernaum:

I tell you most solemnly, unless you eat the flesh of the *Son of Man* and drink his blood, you have no life in you. Whoever eats *my* flesh and drinks *my* blood has eternal life, and *I* will raise him up on the last day. For *my* flesh is real food and *my* blood is real drink. Whoever eats *my* flesh and drinks *my* blood remains in *me*, and *I* in him.... The one who feeds on *me* will live because of *me*.

John 6:53-57

How could Jesus have emphasized any more vehemently the need to focus on his real personhood and presence in this sacrament? So urgently does Jesus consider this existential experience of his very real "com-union" (we abiding in him and he in us) that he goes so far as to link it with both our longed-for rapture and eternal life (see John 6:54).

CHRIST-FOCUS IN PRAYER

An out-of-focus Christianity will likewise distort our prayer life. Without a close relationship with Jesus as a person, our prayer will be nothing more than a long-distance phone call to heaven. Only with an awareness of Jesus' personal and very real presence can we ever get a feel for the Father's awesome goodness and intimate love, for no one goes to the Father except through Jesus (see John 14:6).

Jesus promised his disciples that his resurrection would bring a radical change in their thinking; the truth of God's ongoing personal presence would become a meaningful *reality* for them, a *"realized"* experience: "On that day you will *realize* that I am in my Father, and you are *in me*, and I am *in you*" (Jn 14:20). This very realization is itself a state of profound prayer. In this state, praying becomes a communing with the Lord as an intimate friend. It is a never-boring, joyful, delightfully exciting sharing with the one who said, "I no longer call you servants... I have called you friends, for everything that I learned from my Father I have made known to you" (Jn 15:15).

CHRIST-FOCUS IN SCRIPTURE

I once saw a fascinating copy of the United States Constitution engraved on a copper plate. Close-up, the letters of each word seemed uniform in size and depth. In reality, they were subtly shaded so that if the entire text were held at arm's length, it displayed a strikingly vivid picture of George Washington.

Like this engraved image of Washington, Jesus' presence in Scripture can go unrecognized to those who lack a deep, loving, and *real* relationship with Christ—even if they have a reverence for God's holy Word. But Jesus is truly present in Scripture, as Vatican II affirmed: "He is present in his word... it is he himself who speaks when the holy Scriptures are read."[1]

Our awareness of Christ's vibrant presence in Scripture is enormously heightened by the Holy Spirit through the gift of understanding (see Isaiah 11:2). Though this is not a specifically charismatic gift in itself, understanding is usually more operative in those who have been baptized in the Spirit and have come to know the *reality* of Jesus as Lord of their lives in a dramatically existential way. This is the pentecostal experience that Jesus promised: "When he, the Spirit of truth, comes, he will guide you into all truth... He will bring glory to *me* by taking from what is mine and *making it known to you*" (Jn 16: 13-14).

CHRIST-FOCUS IN SPIRITUAL GROWTH

The practice of virtue is like riding a bicycle: if you stop moving forward, you fall down. It is a fragile state that can be weakened or even shattered by a lapse into worldliness, materialism, resentment, lust, unforgiveness, selfishness, self-pity, or any of a thousand other forms of failure. Whenever this happens, the less mature soul is usually inclined to strive to "get a grip" by exerting more effort or trying some new thing. But such antidotes will never neutralize the inner poison. Though the soul may feel driven to try to stumble frantically along to the heights of holiness, it must instead listen quietly for the Shepherd's voice calling out through the fog of confusion and distraction.

When Jesus' presence seems hopelessly lost, it is all too easy to forget his promise—"I will show *myself* to him" (Jn 14:21)—and his prayer: "Father, I want those you have given me to be *with me* where I am, and to see my glory" (17:24). Striving to recapture the experience of Jesus' companionship, the soul tries to reinflame unaided the dying embers of love; it hardly thinks of Jesus' reminder, "He who loves *me*... I will love" (14:21). It seeks the lost spiritual joy but forgets Jesus' plea "that *my* joy may be in you and that your joy may be complete" (15:11). It strives after its evaporated peace, but the memory of Jesus' peace-promise has also evaporated: "My peace I give you... Do not let your heart be troubled" (14:27).

But all this misplaced striving can only result in frustration. Effort is the wrong antidote to what ails us; Jesus himself is what we need. He is our chair lift to the top of every mountain we may encounter!

God usually speaks to us in whispers, although sometimes he does shout—especially through catastrophes—to get our attention in momentous matters. Some rebellious souls don't respond in compliance but shout back in defiance and anger. Most often, though, God's voice is simply ignored—especially when it comes through those sporadic grace-whispers. It happens so easily, as there are so many other voices competing with God's and luring us into the fripperies of life.

But consider what might happen if we learned to pay attention to these inspirations of grace. For example, perhaps just such a grace-whisper is offered through our reading of the following simple statistic: in any assembly of adults (children and teens excluded), one out of every thirteen persons will be dead within one year.

This statistic may stimulate us to reflection. Which of us will be in eternity a year from now, giving an account of our stewardship to God? What am I doing to prepare for the fact that I *might* be among that eight percent of adults? Now, many persons will allow such a spark of insight to pass by—a spurt of grace that may never impact them again, though they may casually recall it later. But if we are learning to be more responsive to grace, this statistic can have some practical impact on us. We might make some changes in how we use our time, and resolve to devote more of it to Scripture reading, prayer, or a volunteer charity activity. We might decide to do what we can to set our relationships right, forgiving someone who has hurt us, apologizing for hurting another, and so on.

"Since we live by the Spirit," writes Paul, "let us keep in step with the Spirit" (Gal 5:25). That phrase, "keep in step with the Spirit," is threatening to some people; they wrongly think that consistent response to the Spirit's promptings is a pressured form of spirituality. But this misconstrues the whole creature-Creator relationship! It is not a burdensome ordeal to move in lockstep with the Lord by consistently responding to his grace-nudges. The last thing God would want to do is suppress our happy freedom by putting us in a spiritual straitjacket. It is only the abuse of that freedom that we are called to guard against. Real freedom is not license, but freedom to serve God and each other in love (see 1 Peter 2:16 and Galatians 5:13).

Hence, there is no constraint or pressure or compulsion for the person who is always happy to hear the voice of God and is eager to acknowledge it. Each inspiration of grace, each grace-whisper, is a monologue that is meant to draw us into a loving dialogue with him. A friend-to-friend love tryst is not a pressured situation but a delight; the same goes for being faithful in responding to God and walking with him hand-in-hand. As a matter of fact, the more faithful we are in responding to God's graces, the easier and more delightful the habit becomes.

Timing is vital here. In a Christ-focused person the loving response is immediate. There is no grace opportunity that won't take "now" for an answer!

The importance of timing is impressively illustrated in the results of a research study by the Mercedes-Benz car company. It revealed the amazing fact that *nine out of ten* car crashes would be avoided if drivers could hit the brakes *one second* sooner! (Some people have suggested hand brakes on the steering wheel to save that second that costs thousands of lives every year.) In other areas of life too, it is not only time that is important but timing.

Every moment of time given to us in this life is precious, but some moments are more critical than others. The timely eruptions of grace are like geysers—not continuous but sporadic. By God's special providence they are uniquely chosen moments in our life when our soul is God-kissed. The prologue of John's Gospel exults in these many gifts: "From the fullness of his grace we have all received one blessing after another" (Jn 1:16).

CHRIST-FOCUS IN HEALING

To seek healing rather than the divine Healer is one of the most common forms of out-of-focus Christianity. (It is also one of the least recognized and hardest to correct.) People who are suffering severely can easily become distanced from Christ. Their physical pain and emotional suffering are so preoccupying that these people tend to become self-centered. This distorts their spiritual perspective, leading them to seek "it" rather than "him," to plead frantically for healing rather than for a meaningful encounter with the divine Healer.

Jesus had such an encounter with the blind Bartimaeus, who took the first step by acknowledging Jesus as the great "Son of David," while humbly begging for mercy (see Mark 10:46-52). Notice that Jesus then took the initiative. Compassionately, he called Bartimaeus over and gently elicited his request: "What do you want me to do for you?" (10:51). The blind man's subsequent cure was, as Jesus told him, a faith-triggered healing—but his was a faith that focused on Jesus the Healer rather than on the expected healing.

This focus on Jesus is crucial because it provides the only adequate antidote to the poison of great pain and suffering. Then, instead of indulging in querulous complaints, we grow in intimacy with Jesus, which brings, paradoxically, joy and peace. We experience the peace and rest that Jesus promised to the anguished: "Come to *me*, all you who are weary and burdened, and *I* will give you rest. Take *my* yoke upon you and learn from *me*... and you will find rest for your souls. For *my* yoke is easy and *my* burden is light" (Mt 11:28-30). And we can make sense out of Peter's exhortation: "*Rejoice* that you participate in the sufferings of Christ" (1 Pt 4:13).

By focusing on Jesus when we are in pain, we can associate ourselves with his redemptive sufferings. This is how Paul viewed his own sufferings in the service of Christ (see Colossians 1:24), as also his prayers of petition for the salvation of others (see Ephesians 1:16). The kingdom-building power of Paul's sufferings and prayer derived from the awesome experience of being incorporated into Christ (see Ephesians 1:13) and "identified" with him (see Galatians 2:20). Paul lived what Peter wrote, "Since Christ suffered in his body, arm yourselves also with the same attitude" (1 Pt 4:1).

Those who have lost (or never attained) a consistent Christ-focus might do well to reflect on all these areas in which it is vital to have one, and to consider what types of spiritual failure they may be especially vulnerable to. Remember: the only real and ultimate antidote to all spiritual toxins is to keep focused on *"Christ in you, the hope of glory"* (Col 1:27).

FIVE

Obeying God's Will—Gateway to Security

A simple but devout minister in the Ozarks was once challenged by an agnostic tourist. "You say that we should strive to obey God in every way, without question," scoffed the agnostic. "If God asked you to jump through a brick wall, would you do it?"

"Well," drawled the woodlander, "It would be up to me to throw myself at the wall—but it would be up to God to throw me THROUGH it."

In a facetious way, that minister's response reflects an obediential mentality that Paul calls "obedience that comes from faith" (Rom 1:5). It is a faith-engendered response to the "active" aspect of God's will, called his "signified" will. It involves the intent to do whatever God wants one to do, without question or hesitancy. This "active" obedience is the counterpart to the more "passive" response of holy abandonment or surrender to that aspect of God's will called his "good-pleasure" will. Such surrender involves accepting whatever happens in one's life —that is, whatever is caused or permitted by his loving and wise providence—as part of God's "good pleasure." Responding to both the "signified" and the "good-pleasure" will of God is a grace of the Lord, who is often alluded to in this context as the God of peace. "May the God of peace... equip you with everything good for *doing* his will [signified will of God] and work in us *what is pleasing to him* [the good-pleasure will of God]" (Heb 13:21).

Here we will consider only one aspect of conformity to God's will: obedience to his signified will, whether manifested indirectly through a divinely chosen representative or directly through personal guidance from the Lord. Those who exercise the "obedience that comes from faith" in response to God's signified will, enjoy many spiritual advantages. One such benefit, which I will explore briefly, is spiritual security and the peace that accompanies it.

SECURITY IN OBEYING GOD'S REPRESENTATIVES— IT'S A PROMISE!

In the Bolivian jungle, near a missionary outpost, a tiny boy was playing under a tree. Suddenly he heard the missionary priest call to him, "Philip, obey me instantly—get down on your stomach and crawl toward me fast!" Though bewildered, the lad obeyed immediately. After crawling a few yards, he heard another sharp command, "Now stand up and run to me!" The youngster again obeyed, running into the open arms of the priest who then pointed to a fifteen-foot deadly anaconda snake slithering over the branches of the tree under which the boy had been playing.

Just as Philip was saved through his obedience, those who are ready to obey the commands of a wise and all-loving God will enjoy his guidance and protective embrace. In these tumultuous times, when we're often confronted with fears, insecurities, anxieties, afflictions, diseases, accidents, disasters, crime, and evils of all sorts, God's special protection is supremely desirable.

Mercifully, it even includes reversing the threat of punishing tribulations: "Reform your ways; *obey* the Lord your God. Then the Lord will relent and not bring the disaster he has pronounced against you" (Jer 26:13). No wonder that submitting obediently to God's signified will carries the reward of security!

How does God reveal these commands to us? Sometimes they are given indirectly through his chosen representatives. Occasionally, such intermediaries are angelic. God told the Israelites through Moses, "I am sending an angel ahead of you to guard you... My Name is in him. If you listen to all he says and do all that I say, I will be an enemy to your enemies and will oppose those who oppose you" (Ex 23:20-22). The psalmist pleaded: "Teach me to do your will... May your *good spirit* lead me on level ground" (Ps 143:10).

More often God uses authorized *human* instruments to communicate his will and assure his protection to his children. Thus, the prophet Jeremiah assured King Zedekiah: "Obey the Lord by doing what I tell you. Then it will go well with you, and your life will be spared" (Jer 38:20). Paul, as a communicator of God's ordinances, reminded the docile Roman Christians of the Lord's protection from the devil: "Everyone has heard about your obedience.... The God of peace will crush Satan under your feet" (Rom 16:19-20).

Obeying those who represent God is a sure way of knowing and obeying God himself, even when it is through a chain of command: "As the Lord commanded his servant Moses, so Moses commanded Joshua, and Joshua did it; he left nothing undone of all that the *Lord* commanded Moses" (Jos 11:15). In obeying the orders of any legitimate human authorities (we must not obey sinful orders, of course), it is ultimately to God that we are submitting; "keeping *God's* commands is what counts" (1 Cor 7:19), for that is what conveys his promised protection. Thus James, acting as God's instrument, prescribes many ordinances; yet he promises protection from the devil for those whose submission is oriented not to himself but to God: "Submit yourselves to *God*... the devil will flee from you" (Jas 4:7).

Even Jesus submitted to the Father's will as expressed through God's intermediary, John the Baptist. He was baptized—an act of humble obedience which was endorsed by the Spirit of God descending on him as a dove, and by the Father's thundering approval from the heavens: "This is my Son, whom I love; with him I am well pleased" (Mt 3:17). Only after this do we see Jesus overcoming Satan's temptations and vanquishing him during their encounter in the desert.

Peace and security thrive among those who obey God's will as expressed through legitimate human authority. Joshua obeyed Moses' orders and won monumental military victories that led to peace for his people: "The land had rest from war" (Jos 11:23). And even soul-rest comes to those who seek to do God's will. "Ask where the good way is, and walk in it," Jeremiah counseled, "and you will find rest for your souls" (Jer 6:16).

WHO DETERMINES GOD'S WILL FOR US TODAY?

This is a question that deserves our close consideration, in view of the importance of God's will for our temporal and eternal security. For the answer we must take a quick look at how God has chosen to work among human beings.

After redeeming the human race, the incarnate Son of God wanted to perpetuate the reality of his great redemptive act in future generations. He established a new covenant with the men and women he had redeemed, who became known as Christians. He gathered them into a Church where they could find order, security, and strength; he knew that this kind of structure would be needed—just as a body needs a skeleton, without which it would collapse in a heap of flesh and skin. He established his Church on a "rock foundation" and even renamed its first leader to make the point: Simon became Peter, which means rock. "On this rock I will build my Church," he then solemnly proclaimed (Mt 16:18).

To this internal security Jesus added external protection by endowing the Church with the strength to repel the onslaughts of the evil one. "The gates of hell will not prevail against it" (Mt 16:18). Immediately after conferring this double security, he granted to the new leader of the new Church the awesome authority to formulate laws that would articulate God's will for its members: "I will give you the keys of the kingdom of heaven; whatever you bind on earth will be bound in heaven, and whatever you loose on earth will be loosed in heaven" (Mt 16:19). Jesus then authenticated his actions by alluding to his divine messiahship (see Matthew 16:20), thereby reminding his apostles, the new hierarchy, that he had the power to grant such authority.

Finally, after commanding his followers to expand this Church by "making disciples of all nations," Jesus added a final commission, another security measure: "teaching them to *obey everything I have commanded you*" (Mt 28:19-20). Obedience to God's Church, along with obedience to God's Word, now provided a double measure of security for his people.

With this magnificent arrangement, God's people received a special kind of security, inasmuch as they could now know God's will clearly and precisely. Furthermore, this security was to last for all time, since Jesus promised to send the Holy Spirit to guide the Church "into all truth" (Jn 16:13) and to remain with it himself "to the very end of the age" (Mt 28:20).

The implications of Jesus' promise are positively overwhelming. It means that even today Jesus speaks to us clearly of God's "signified" will for us in countless matters, not only through his revealed words in sacred Scripture but also through the Church that he founded. Personally commissioning the seventy-two disciples as the Church's earliest hierarchy (see Luke 10:1), Jesus established their vicarious authority: "He who listens to you listens to me; he who rejects you rejects me" (10:16).

John, one of the apostles who first received this God-commissioned authority, wrote in his first epistle: "We are from God, and whoever knows God listens to us; but whoever is not from God does not listen to us. This is how we recognize the Spirit of truth and the spirit of falsehood" (1 Jn 4:6). John, of course, could attribute the spirit of falsehood to those who rejected God's will and truth found in the Church's teaching, because he had heard Jesus say, "If anyone refuses to listen to the church, treat him as you would a pagan" (Mt 18:17)—that is, as not authentically Christian.

Clearly, God has chosen to present his will for us through his Church in matters of both doctrine (things to be believed) and discipline (things to be practiced or avoided). And according to his revealed Word, God intends to convey his will not only by his continued spiritual presence down through time but also down through the Church's continued chain of command, through the bishops and pastors he delegates (as, in earlier times, he delegated authority through others: from Moses to Joshua, for example, and from Joshua to his field commanders—see Joshua 11:15).

Because of the higher authority they represent, all God-commissioned shepherds deserve respect: "Respect those who work hard among you, *who are over you in the Lord,* and who admonish you. Hold them in highest regard for their work" (1 Thes 5:12-13).

Scripture shows that the subjects' obedience and the shepherds' accountability are correlative: "*Obey your leaders* and submit to their authority. They keep watch over you as *men who must give an account.* Obey them so that their work will be a joy, not a burden" (Heb 13:17).

Occasionally, of course, there are leaders who abuse their authority, either by unjust or malicious commands, or by ignorance or error in doctrinal matters. But all shepherds, whom "the Holy Spirit has made overseers" (Acts 20:28), will be held severely accountable to God if they should ever bastardize their sacred authority: "I am against those shepherds and I will hold them accountable for my flock" (Ez 34:10).

Meanwhile, there is security in knowing that God's will is not violated when we obey unjust but *non-sinful* commands (Acts

5:29) or when we disregard *obviously* erroneous teachings (Gal 1:8). There is also security in knowing that the Church itself and its chief shepherd enjoy doctrinal infallibility, "coextensive with the deposit of revelation" (Vatican II: *Lumen Gentium*, art. 25) and granted by Jesus himself (see Matthew 16:17-19; 18:18).

And so even in this modern age, Jesus truly speaks to us—for he promised to be with us always—and delineates with remarkable explicitness his will for us in countless matters. He does this through all the regulations and revisions in canon law and liturgical law, through the documents of ecumenical councils, and through papal proclamations on issues such as priestly celibacy, artificial birth control, the male priesthood, Marian devotion, marriage requirements, and obligations regarding receiving the sacraments.

We should have a consummate respect for all the mandates of the gospel message, as well as for all Old Testament ordinances that are still current under the new covenant. With equal respect we must also lovingly and joyfully accept the Church's rules, regulations, and teachings, while being grateful for the security of knowing that God's will is clearly revealed in all these norms. If we are "cafeteria Catholics" who choose only the beliefs that suit us, we are not in God's will. And if we deny or reject God's will thus expressed, we are praying hypocritically when we plead, "Thy will be done on earth as it is in heaven."

Of course, *salvation* is not essentially the result of good works such as acts of obedience to God's law, although our obedience does dispose us for it. Jesus "became the source of *salvation* to all who *obey* him" (Heb 5:9), and "the man who does the will of God lives forever" (1 Jn 2:17). Our *sanctification*, however, is directly related to how we obey God's will. "If anyone obeys his word, *God's love is truly made complete in him,*" John tells us. "This is how we know we are in him" (1 Jn 2:5). In other words, those who strive to fulfill God's will perfectly move rapidly toward spiritual maturity.

GOD DOESN'T SHOUT—HE WHISPERS

So far we have considered only the indirect ways in which God expresses his signified will for us to obey. But he also manifests that same signified will directly, through personal guidance revealed to each of us in many ways.

Very few people can think of even one time in their life when they heard God directly and clearly give them a word of command. Often our own lack of spiritual sensitivity is the problem. Yet by analyzing situations in which God has directly and clearly conveyed his will to more privileged souls, we can glean certain principles that will help us to discern and fulfill his will.

Let us take a look at Acts 16:6-10. Here is an example of a clear exposition of God's will to the pioneers of the early Church. Paul, with Silas and Timothy, was on a missionary trip in the region of Phrygia and Galatia, "having been kept by the Holy Spirit from preaching the word in the province of Asia." Later, "they tried to enter Bithynia, but the Spirit of Jesus would not allow them to." Obediently redirecting their steps, they went down to Troas, where Paul had a vision of a man of Macedonia begging for help. He deduced that "God had called us to preach the gospel to them." This story of divine guidance illustrates several principles that we would do well to bear in mind as we seek God's will in our own lives.

God always manifests his will while we are moving toward a goal, even if that goal is not always pre-defined. When the Lord altered their itinerary, these missionaries didn't quit and go home. They continued to pursue their goal, while allowing God to zig-zag their route. A ship that is moored cannot be piloted; a car that is parked cannot be steered. Only as we move in the current of the Holy Spirit are we given guidance in God's will. A stagnant soul, waiting to be pushed by God, may have an endless wait.

We must always be prepared to hear God speak to us in any of many means, most of them not charismatically dramatic. The precise way in which the Spirit blocked the journey of Paul and his companions is not described in this passage. It may have been through visions (the man from Macedonia), providential circumstances, a charism of discernment or prophecy, or by simple common sense divinely enhanced by a special "intuition."

Divine guidance is always God-initiated. Like Paul and his companions, we may start out with a plan that we *believe* to be the will of God—which is any plan that can comfortably be lined up with God's word. In the absence of any specific directions, we should continue to do what we know is to be done: cooking, shopping, working, and so on. Any change of agenda should come from God, who can easily affect the direction of our plans through a change of circumstances. These changes are sometimes pleasant, such as a "chance" meeting with an old friend or an unexpected kindness from a stranger. Other times, these "changes" come from a less-pleasant source: traffic jams, bankruptcies, earthquakes, family illnesses, and job losses. Whatever happens, the bottom line is Romans 8:28: *"In all things* God works for the good of those who love him, who have been called according to his purpose"—that is, *those who respond to the call of his purposed will for them.*

We will not hear God's voice unless we listen prayerfully for it. Paul and Silas "looked for a place of prayer" as they traveled. Communing with God (that is, prayer) requires the stillness of a prayer-saturated soul. This is why a contemplative person is more attuned to God's will than one whose prayer is "chattering with the Lord." Non-stop talkers seldom hear others.

Prayer is not talking *to* God, but talking *with* him—and that implies listening. During the Transfiguration, Peter was blathering excitedly about his plans to memorialize the event with three shrines, when the Father's voice from heaven thundered, "This is my beloved Son. *Listen* to him!" (Mt 17:5). Peter's plans for shrines on Mount Tabor were not God's plans. Because he wasn't listening, his fervent plans dead-ended in oblivion. Many of our sincere endeavors to do God's will also end up in the garbage heap of human failure because we haven't learned to listen prayerfully.

Divine proddings seldom come to us by visions or locutions. Far more often God speaks his will by reminding us, in particular situations, to act—or react—with heroic kindness and patience, with love and forgiveness; he inspires us to find creative ways to express concern for others as we plod through this vale of tears.

I recall asking myself one time what I had done that particular day to make this a better world. Ashamed at having to answer, "nothing," I asked the Lord to inspire me to do one simple act that would be in accord with his will. The thought came to me that I might call a depressed client I had counseled. It turned out that when she answered the phone, she was holding a pill bottle, preparing to commit suicide by overdose. My call came just in time to lift her depression and save her life.

If we are listening and responding to God, we will recognize that such inspirations are too holy to have been initiated by us; they are graces divinely whispered into our soul. Each response to God's will brings us to a higher level of spiritual security, and our feeling of peace and security increases as we snuggle ever closer into the warm embrace of God's love. Our response to each tiny whisper of God's Spirit is a precious act of virtue that rachets our soul to the next rung on the ladder reaching heavenward. Each brings a surge of growth in holiness. And after all, holiness—union with God—is the ultimate goal we seek in pursuing his will.

As a capstone to these reflections on obeying God's will, I offer this passage from a book by James Leen, *By Jacob's Well:*

The divine will... is an immense storehouse. The present moment lived in the spirit of faith and love is the key of entry. When the soul enters the threshold it finds limitless treasures. To lay hold of this truth is to discover a path which leads straight to God. It is to discover, from morning until evening, in the commonplace happenings of life, numberless opportunities for accumulating spiritual treasure. These acts may be extremely ordinary and trivial in outward appearance.

The constant recognition that they are God's demands on us develops that tender thoughtfulness toward God and toward one's fellows for the love of God. It might appear to the soul itself that it is offering to God the merest trifles, but it does not appear so to God. They are most precious in his eyes.[1]

If we keep this simple truth in sight, we will remain in peace and security throughout our earthly life as we journey toward the eternal peace of heaven.

SIX

Thought Control: Architect of Character

It had to happen sooner or later. A book was published without any words except the title. It was called The Nothing Book. *The New York publishing company that produced it was sued for plagiarism by a Belgian publishing company that had published a similar non-book called* Memoirs of an Amnesiac. *The court decided that blankness was in the public domain and not subject to litigation. So a rash of other blank books flooded the market, such as one titled,* What I Know about Wall Street after 14 Years' Experience.

While blank pages are possible, a totally blank mind is not, outside of dreamless sleep or coma. Scientists tell us that every thought we think leaves its impression on the cortex of the brain. Both helpful and hurtful thoughts can be registered more or less permanently by repetition. If a person thinks the same thought constantly, the impression becomes a mental rut, just as a scratch on a piece of wood gets deeper if a nail is drawn repeatedly over it. In this way habitual thought-patterns are established that are increasingly difficult to reroute. For good or ill, mental ruts (affecting thought patterns) can give rise to emotional ruts (affecting personality), and even to biochemical ruts (affecting health) and behavioral ruts (affecting character). The classic aphorism of Proverbs 23:7 captures this idea: "As a man thinks within himself, so is he."

Both the body and the mind are affected by our thoughts. The science of psychoneuroimmunology (PNI) has demonstrated that the mind interacts psychosomatically with the body by means of at least sixty kinds of neuropeptides—brain chemicals having related "cousins" with neuroreceptors in cells throughout the body. For instance, it is possible that one peptide called "substance P" may be the culprit in asthma and arthritis. Sustained arousal of negative emotions has also been found to activate endocrine hormone secretion and interacting peptides to play a role in cancers, heart attacks, strokes, and slow wound healings. Clearly, sustained emotions like resentment, hatred, depression, and anxiety can undermine physical health.

THE MIND OF CHRIST—THAT'S THE SPIRIT

The flip side of this coin is that positive emotions like love, joy, or hope can benefit both our emotional and bodily health. More importantly, they can upgrade our spiritual health by disposing us to receive the Spirit's grace-activated virtues and gifts to enhance our character, prayer life, and spiritual growth. As the Thomistic theological axiom puts it, "Grace builds on nature."

For instance, as we grow in love, joy, peace, and other fruits of the Spirit, Christ-like thought patterns are engendered. "Remain in *my* love... that *"my* joy may be in you," Jesus says (Jn 15:9, 11). "*My* peace I give you" (Jn 14:27). And Paul urges us to "let the peace *of Christ* rule *in your hearts*" (Col 3:15). We know that these Christic thought patterns are attainable for "those who are being made holy," as the Letter to the

Hebrews calls us. The same passage continues: "The Holy Spirit testifies... 'I will put my laws *in their hearts* and I will write them *on their minds*'" (Heb 10:14-16). When emotions and thoughts are grace-suffused, they are uplifted, so that we begin to "think with the mind of Christ" (1 Cor 2:16).

A rock can be a stepping stone or a stumbling block. The sun can soften wax or harden clay; heat can soften a potato or harden an egg. A grindstone can either polish a stone or grind it to dust. Likewise, our thoughts can be either a help or a hindrance to us spiritually, depending on our spiritual focus. "The mind of the sinful man is death," Paul reminds us, "but the mind controlled by the Spirit is life and peace" (Rom 8:6). And this peace which comes from the Spirit secures our thoughts and emotions, for "the peace of God, which transcends all understanding, will *guard your hearts and your minds* in Christ Jesus" (Phil 4:7).

CAPTIVATING THOUGHTS MADE CAPTIVE

But before our feelings and thoughts (hearts and minds) can be guarded, they must be taken captive. We must "take captive every thought to make it obedient to Christ" (2 Cor 10:5). Only in this way can the very center of our being become fully subject to the lordship of Jesus.

Thoughts are enormously powerful—more than we usually realize. In a moral context, repeated thoughts will either reinforce our friendship with God or nudge us into an alliance with Satan. In a social context, grace-enriched thoughts tend to nourish the wholesome aspects of our human relationships, while morbid thinking poisons them. Our thoughts will inevitably impact our behavior and speech, as Jesus affirmed: "The good man brings good things out of the good stored up in his heart, and the evil man brings evil things out of the evil stored up in his heart. Out of the overflow of his heart his mouth speaks" (Lk 6:45).

Rogue thoughts are loose cannons on the deck. Judas had a

rogue thought—betraying Christ for a handful of silver—and his name became immortalized in infamy. Cain harbored a jealous thought and he slew Abel, committing the world's first murder. Samson nursed lustful thoughts of a harlot, and an entire nation suffered as a result. Haman was obsessed with the thought of hanging Mordecai, but instead he himself was hanged.

Though they may not always lead directly to physical death, thought patterns from the enemy are always destructive. Worry, resentment, doubts, lust, and other such thoughts are emotionally and often physically harmful. Fear plagues many people, often in the form of gripping phobias. Yet these damaging thoughts can be neutralized if we take them captive for Christ.

For example, Scripture tells us 365 times, in various ways, to "fear not," since "the one who fears is not made perfect in love" (1 Jn 4:18). (Here, of course, John is referring to a morbid fear of punishment from God—not to the gift of fear of the Lord, which is a reverent dread of offending God.) Fear-dissolving trust in the Lord must become a virtuous thought-habit.

Worry is another destructive thought pattern, and Jesus condemns it five times in the sixth chapter of Matthew. When we "take it captive to make it obedient to Christ," anxious worry is transformed into a calm and prayerful concern for God's will.

Or frenetic distraction may be our problem. If so, we must turn gently inward to the Lord. Gradually, we will find these troublesome thoughts replaced by a stillness of soul, a tranquil prayer of the mind—a grace-filled awareness of the presence of God: "Be still and know that I am God" (Ps 46:10).

CHANGING YOUR MIND

Under Christ any destructive pattern can be changed into a spiritually uplifting one. Thought patterns that have troubled you for years can be transformed by God's power, beginning right at this moment. If you allow this to happen, your very lifestyle will change accordingly and you will enjoy a great sense of liberation, for "if the Son sets you free, you will be free indeed" (Jn 8:36).

How do you enter into this new freedom? "Put off your old self, which is being corrupted by its deceitful desires," says Paul. *"Be made new in the attitude of your minds...* put on the new self, created to be like God in true righteousness and holiness" (Eph 4:22-23). Chapters four and five of the Letter to the Ephesians elaborate on this advice; they present a sort of program for cooperating with God in acquiring behavior changes by wisely "making the most of every opportunity, because the days are evil" (Eph 5:16).

Paul's program for the Ephesians focuses on changing behavior patterns in order to change thought patterns. Elsewhere, however, he proposes a reverse program: changing thought patterns in order to change behavior patterns. In a brilliant passage in chapter four of his Letter to the Philippians, Paul lists positive thought-patterns and then urges his readers to externalize them by putting them into practice. His suggested litany of thought-patterns, if practiced habitually, is sure to lead to a life of moral and spiritual excellence. Let us take a closer look at this scriptural program for mental and emotional discipline.

A PILOT PROGRAM FOR THE POWER
OF POSITIVE THINKING

> Whatever is true, whatever is noble, whatever is right, whatever is pure, whatever is lovely, whatever is admirable—if anything is excellent or praiseworthy—*think about such things.*
>
> **Philippians 4:8**

"Whatever is true." "God our Savior wants all to come to the knowledge of truth" (1 Tm 2:4); that is why he revealed it. Only those things found explicitly or implicitly in divine revelation can be regarded as reliably true. Though we are usually

unaware of it, this vast array of truths seeps into us as we immerse ourselves in God's Word. When we breathe the spirit of the prophets, pray the lyrics of the psalmist, and ponder the gospel truths with Paul, the Bible becomes a part of us; it inevitably finds expression in our many daily decisions and behavior. Prayerful thinking about sublime truths will result in high-minded habits.

"Whatever is noble." Noble thoughts transcend pettiness—and where pettiness is transcended, there is no conflict. "What causes fights and quarrels?" asks James. "Don't they come from desires that battle within you?" (Jas 4:1). Noble thoughts are the parents of peace. This insight, if lived out, would empty our divorce courts.

"Whatever is right." To *do* only what is right, we must be continually *conscious* of what is right. God *inspired* Abraham "to keep the way of the Lord, by *doing* what is right and just" (Gn 18:19). Having an eschatalogical mind-set can help us here. By this I mean being aware of the nearness of salvation. If we can think about the present time as it relates to the end times, this thought will remind us to "put aside the deeds of darkness" and "behave decently" (Rom 13:12-13). Just thinking of the "thief-in-the-night" surprise of the second coming of Christ, Paul implies, is enough to keep us on the right track.

"Whatever is pure." Peter wrote his two epistles "to stimulate you to wholesome [pure] thinking" (2 Pt 3:1). James remarked that "wisdom that comes from heaven is first of all pure" (Jas 3:17). Jesus stressed the importance of purity by attaching a promise for the pure of heart in the Beatitudes: "they will see God" (Mt 5:8). In his own way, the psalmist grasped this truth too: "Who may stand in his [God's] holy place? He who has clean hands and a pure heart" (Ps 24:3-4; see also 73:1).

Biblical writers refer to the heart as the center of the human spirit. From it spring emotions, thoughts, motivations, and, ultimately, action. That is why Solomon considered mental self-discipline so important: it keeps the heart pure and uncontaminated like a life-giving water well. "Above all else, guard your heart," he urged, "for it is the wellspring of life" (Prv 4:23).

"Whatever is lovely." "Lovely," as used in Scripture, means lovable, charming, winsome, or pleasant. "He is altogether lovely," exults the beloved in the Song of Songs (Sg 5:16). Obviously, she is focused on her lover's fascinating qualities! Though this verse refers to a nuptial type of relationship, its focus on the positive is something from which all our relationships can benefit. True Christian love—charity—is much easier to practice when we learn to see other people's qualities and strengths more than their weak points and failings, to *habitually* think positive and "lovely" thoughts about people rather than negative ones.

And have you ever noticed that those who are the most loving are themselves the most lovable? There is a cyclic dynamic at work here, to be sure. Nothing makes you more "lovely" than thinking "lovely" thoughts of others.

"Whatever is admirable, excellent, or praiseworthy." Paul presents a basic guideline on this subject: "If you owe respect, pay respect; if honor, then honor" (Rom 13:7). The Bible offers many examples of admirable and praiseworthy persons and encourages us to give honor where honor is due. Ruth is described as a "woman of noble character" (Ru 3:11) and is praised for her kindness. The devout Jew Ananias (see Acts 22:12) and also Cornelius, the Gentile centurion, were "respected by all the Jewish people" (Acts 10:22). Paul urges respect and admiration for church leaders, "holding them in the highest regard in love" (1 Thes 5:12-13). Titus and his companion apparently received this high regard from the local churches (see 2 Corinthians 8:17-18).

Not just in the Bible but all around us are people who should stir our praise and admiration. For example, this verse from Proverbs might call to mind some of the women we have encountered in our lives: "A woman who fears the Lord is to be praised... Let her works bring her praise" (Prv 31:31). Since women as a group have tended to be under-esteemed, this might be a good place to start focusing the spotlight of praise. Other possibilities are dedicated and faith-filled young people, lay missionaries, or volunteer workers in your parish. You may know of others who inspire you by their examples of faith-in-action.

Catholics also venerate the saints out of respect and admiration for their heroic virtue, such as the humble repentance of Mary Magdalen. Foremost among these is Mary, the mother of Jesus, who was praised as "blessed among all women" by both the archangel Gabriel and Elizabeth, her relative (Lk 1:28, 42). Mary foretold that all generations would call her blessed, in holy admiration for her God-given graces (1:48); so too, generations of believers admired the ancients for their great faith (see Hebrews 11:2; 11:39).

Truly, "we are surrounded by a great cloud of witnesses," both in heaven and on earth (Heb 12:1). By their excellence and praiseworthy holiness, all of them excite us to uplifting thoughts of admiration that ultimately focus admiringly on God himself. Cultivating such praise-thinking is itself praiseworthy.

THE BEST OUTLOOK IS AN UPLOOK

Perhaps you have heard this popular couplet penned by Frederick Langbudge:

"Two men looked out from prison bars;
One saw mud, the other, stars."

The uplook mentality is what Paul advises for the Colossians: "Set your *hearts* on things above.... Set your *minds* on things above, not on earthly things.... Clothe yourselves with compassion, kindness, humility, gentleness and patience. Bear with each other, forgive.... And over all these virtues put on love, which binds them all together.... Let the peace of Christ rule *in your hearts*(Col 3:1-15).

What we look at and think about does have a big effect on

us. In cybernetic jargon, the acronym GIGO is often used; it stands for "Garbage In, Garbage Out"—erroneous input into a computer results in erroneous output. So it is with our minds. If we fill them with the garbage of sleazy literature or questionable television programs and films; if we welcome worldly conversation or thoughts of envy, jealousy, avarice, pride, morbid fear, resentment, and so on—then we leave little or no room for God to work in us. When our outlook is not an "uplook" but a "downlook," we're not honestly facing God to let him work in us.

God "knows your hearts," Jesus told the Jews (Lk 16:15), and he knows ours too. He sees what we need and he wants to give it to us: "a spirit of power, of love, and of self-discipline" (2 Tm 1:7)—especially in the area of our thoughts.

DON'T CHANGE YOURSELF—LET GOD DO IT.

"Make every effort to add... to your knowledge *self-control*" (2 Pt 1:5-6). The effort that Peter speaks of here is not a strenuous exertion but a firm intention to maintain a Godward gaze. By this means we learn to "hold on to the good and avoid every kind of evil" (1 Thes 5:21-22; see Romans 12:9). The mistake we usually make is trying to change ourselves—but that approach is doomed to failure. Instead, we must allow ourselves to be changed. The secret is to do this through the "passive activity" described in 2 Corinthians 3:18: *"reflect* the Lord's glory, being transformed into his likeness, with ever-increasing glory, which comes from the Lord, who is the Spirit."

The glory of Christ that we must mirror is in our character; hence we can substitute the word *character* for *glory* in Paul's statement. We must let the Spirit change us, almost in spite of ourselves, to mirror Christ's character to those around us. To open ourselves to this transformation, we must make Jesus our constant companion. Even five minutes in a heart-to-heart encounter with him will transform our entire day; it will change our thoughts and feelings, and enable us to do things for him that we would never have attempted otherwise. Conscious of the presence of Jesus, we become docile to his teaching, as he instructs us to be more charitable, patient, and "meek and humble of heart" (Mt 11:29). We catch the spirit as his character is mirrored more and more in our behavior.

If Christians were determined enough to reject contaminating influences and let their thoughts become totally Christ-patterned, this corrupt world could become a Garden of Eden right now! We Christians could tip the scales and lift the world to a new high, in spite of the negative thoughts of others around us. But this cannot happen unless we habitually direct our thoughts (which affect our actions) to Christlike ideals rather than to worldly ones.

THE CHOICE IS YOURS

You and I have been gifted with the precious benefit of a free will. God lets us choose to grow spiritually as much as we want. If things seem dark for you at the moment, you don't have to leave them that way. You can change, and you can do it now. You can choose to let the Lord free you from worry, resentment, morbid brooding, self-pity, or dark desires. But this can happen only if you yield yourself totally to the Lord, to be made whole by him, "in body, mind, and spirit" (1 Thes 5:23).

It requires generous cooperation with God's grace to bring thoughts and emotions into line with God's magnificent plan. But as we learn to practice thought-control, the master architect of our character, we will be fitted by the Master Architect for life in the celestial mansion that he has designed to be our home.

PART II

Stamina for the Spiritual Journey

Frustrated by slow-and-go freeway traffic on my way to a television interview, I decided to try a shortcut by surface streets with which I was unfamiliar. My frustration was compounded by frequent stop lights, cul-de-sacs, and a labyrinth of zig-zag, curved, and dead-end streets. Breathless, I arrived barely in time for the live telecast—to the great relief of the host and cameramen. I resolved never again to use shortcuts when a time risk or safety risk might be involved.

There are no safe or time-saving shortcuts to holiness. Time, effort, and a persistent struggle are required, though always under the aegis of divine grace. Holy living is a daily battle against the world, the devil, and the flesh. Our successes encourage us and, providentially, our failures humble us. Finally, like Paul, we come to see ourselves as "not having a righteousness of my own… but the righteousness that comes from God and is by faith" (Phil 3:9). And if we follow Paul's lead, we know never to rest on our laurels: "Straining toward what is ahead," he says, "I press on toward the goal" (Phil 3:14).

So far we have been looking at the relational aspect of spirituality; that is, a human creature's loving relationship with his or her Creator. Now we turn our attention to another facet of the spiritual life, God's along-the-way encouragements for our journey to him.

In addition to his ever-present grace, God provides countless such reinforcements along the way. They include his inerrant word in Scripture; the example of Mary, his masterpiece of creation; the supportive companionship of a personally assigned guardian angel; and even the exhilarating feeling of spiritual accomplishment—the fruit of the Spirit that is joy, which has been called "the outcome of the harmonious development of the virtues." All of these helps are part of God's design for strengthening and comforting us.

Those of Irish descent will recall the Gaelic farewell that is almost a benediction. It seems to summarize the various godsends along the road to holiness that are canvassed in this section: "May the face of the good news and the back of the bad news be always in front of you; and may the good Lord keep you in the palm of his hand and never close his fist!"

SEVEN

Amazing Grace— Your Expandable Quota of Divine Life

An ancient oriental fable tells of a tiny fish that overheard a guru at the river bank teaching his disciples about the life-sustaining importance of water. "If it is that important," mused the little fish, "I must find some of this thing called water, or I'll soon die."

He began asking the other fish in the river about water, but none of them seemed to know anything about it. Finally a wise old fish told the little fish that he had been surrounded by water all his life, and that his very life was being sustained by water at that moment. "Enjoy the water," advised the older fish, "appreciate it and draw on it to continue living and thriving."

Like the little fish, the Samaritan woman at the well knew little about abundant, freely available, life-giving and life-sustaining water. Her ignorance, though, was not about ordinary water, but about the "living water" that Jesus offered. He called it a "gift of God" (Jn 4:10) and described it as not only satisfying but also vital for fulfilling one's very destiny: "Whoever drinks the water I give him will never suffer thirst. Indeed, the water I give him will become in him a spring of water welling up to eternal life" (Jn 4:14).

Jesus alone can offer this gift: "If anyone is thirsty, let him come to *me* and drink" (Jn 7:37). While persons who are not thirsty for this water can still receive it (infants at baptism, for example), those with an appreciative "thirst for righteousness" (Mt 5:6) will seek to increase their supply by purposefully going to Jesus, whose gracious invitation echoes Isaiah 55:1: "Come, all you who are thirsty, come to the waters."

What precisely is this redoubtable, awesome "living water"? It is grace—the very life of God himself within us, enabling us to "participate in the divine nature" (2 Pt 1:4). It is a kind of projection of God's august presence into us, which is spiritually both life-giving and life-sustaining, for it entails "everything we need for both life and godliness" (2 Pt 1:3). A supernatural gift (one that transcends our human nature), it is aptly described as "Amazing Grace"—as in the title of the popular hymn by the sailor-turned-clergyman, John Newton.

The New Testament Greek word for this great gift is *charis.* This is a word with multiple meanings, although it is typically translated "grace" in about 130 out of the roughly 160 times it is used. This more common meaning is found especially in the epistles of Paul, who championed the Christian doctrine of grace.

According to the Scripture scholar Joseph Thayer, grace, as used in the New Testament, is a refinement of the Hebrew word that means God's "favor," "blessing," or "goodwill." He defines grace as "kindness by which God freely bestows favors even upon the non-deserving, grants to sinners pardon, and offers them eternal salvation through Christ." Thus gifted by Christ with this God-presence, the soul is enriched with God-like qualities; it shares in God's gifts and blessings, as well as his sin-free state and his eternal life.

The greatest theological expositor of grace, St. Thomas Aquinas, taught that grace is fundamentally God's gracious love echoed back to him from the graced person by that person's response in thought, word, and act. Bestowed as grace, God's love confers on the soul a quota of God's own life and holiness. This makes the soul pleasing to God. As children can resemble their parents, children of God better resemble God when they are filled with grace. And so, the supply of grace we receive is the very grace of the Father dwelling in Jesus that is extended to us by the Holy Spirit.

"Amazing grace," indeed! God doesn't just "order a piece of pie" for us, so to speak; he keeps giving us big pieces of his own limitless "pie." The Gospel of John puts it more elegantly: "From his fullness of have we all received, grace upon grace" (Jn 1:16, RSV).

Look again at this phrase, "grace upon grace." Doesn't it conjure up a picture of graces being piled up, like gifts stacked into someone's open arms? For instance, the grace of *being* righteous is added to the grace of *becoming* righteous. As the Council of Trent explained about this sequence, we are unable to move ourselves to repent of serious sin; it is God's "prevenient," or "actual," grace that entices us to repent. If we do accede to this nudge from God and repent, then a subsequent grace of holiness—"sanctifying" grace—is bestowed. (This process is sometimes called justification, or being made just.)

Many divine interventions involve similar grace sequences. The most common is the one illustrated above: actual grace leading to sanctifying grace. (Actual grace and sanctifying grace are biblical *concepts*, but as technical *terms* they are derived from medieval theology.) Sanctifying grace is also called "habitual" grace because it inhabits, or stays habitually in, the soul that is uncontaminated with serious sin. In this it differs from actual grace, which affects the soul only momentarily by prompting the intellect to a helpful insight, or motivating the will to do good or avoid evil.

An analogy may be helpful here. A car with a dead battery can't start itself, but it can be jump-started by being linked to another car with a live battery. Once the disabled car is started, it needs something more to keep it going: gasoline, sustained firing of the spark plugs to activate the pistons, and so on. Likewise, God's gratuitous offer to jump-start into divine life a soul dead in sin is an actual (actualizing) grace. The sinner who accepts this spiritual jumper cable link-up is disposed for the subsequent sanctifying grace. Like the car that springs to life and then moves forward, engine running and gears engaged, the soul becomes alive in holiness and is made capable of growing in holiness. In all this, clearly, "it is God who works in you to will and to act according to his good purpose" (Phil 2:13).

Sometimes the grace sequence is multiple. Imagine for a moment that you are a slave on the auction block. The highest bidder pays the price for you and then announces that you are no longer a slave but a free person. That is an analogy of the grace of redemption which, when received, is called the grace of salvation, or conversion. This grace of salvation induces further actual graces, which in turn foster sanctifying grace. Paul describes this three-step sequence: "The *grace of God* that brings salvation has appeared to all men. It teaches us to say 'No' to ungodliness and worldly passions, and to live self-controlled, upright and godly lives" (Ti 2: 11-12).

Now suppose that after being emancipated from slavery you become a criminal and are awaiting a death sentence for a crime. But you are astonished to learn that the governor has pardoned you. You are not only emancipated (redeemed) but also acquitted (forgiven). This situation is analogous to God's grace of redemption (salvation), followed by the grace of forgiveness (actualized by repentance); and this is followed by even more spiritual gifts or graces. Again, Paul delineates this multiple sequence: "In Christ we have *redemption* and *forgiveness* by the riches of *God's grace,* lavished on us with wisdom and understanding" (Eph 1:7).

Like a donation to a homeless person, grace is given to us by God gratuitously. There is no way we could earn it, even if we wanted to, and no way we could deserve it. "It is by grace you have been saved," Paul stresses, "through faith—and this not from yourselves, it is the gift of God—not by works, so that no one can boast" (Eph 2:8-9). Yet we have a say in how grace affects us: we can use it, misuse it, refuse it, or lose it. If a street person carelessly loses the money given him or wastes it on drugs or liquor, the donor is disappointed. So too, we must not squander God's precious gift of grace but foster it, as Paul's impassioned exhortation directs: "We urge you not to receive God's grace in vain" (2 Cor 6:1).

Almost as amazing as grace itself is the indifference that some people show toward it. Even many Christians today are walking around half-dead because they receive God's life-gift half-heartedly. Other people reject it outright, as Isaiah noted: "Though grace is shown to the wicked, they go on doing evil" (Is 26:10).

St. Augustine identified an essential element for receiving grace: "God gives where he finds empty hands." When our hands are full of baubles, how can we possibly receive other gifts? If we are burdened with worldly interests, we will be poorly disposed to receive bountiful graces from the beneficent hand of God. "Anyone who chooses to be a friend of the world becomes an enemy of God," James cautions, going on to cite a proverb that expresses the consequences of our choices: "God opposes the proud but give grace to the humble" (Jas 4:4, 6; Prv 3:34). C.S. Lewis makes a similar point in his book, *Mere Christianity:*

> God shows much more of himself to some people than to others—not because he has favorites, but because it is impossible for him to show himself to a person whose whole mind and character are in the wrong condition. Sunlight, though it has no favorites, cannot be reflected in a dusty mirror as clearly as in a clean one.[1]

If only we could see "the incomparable riches of his grace" (Eph 2:7) that rain down upon each of us in manifold forms every day and hour! Then, like thirsty nomads in a desert cloud-burst, we would strive to catch every drop of this amazing grace from the loving heart of God, and we would "continue to grow in the grace of God" (Acts 13:43). Nothing would delight God more, for he wishes always to extend his benevolence: "to make *all* grace abound to you, so that in *all* things at *all* times, having *all* that you need, you will abound in *every* good work" (2 Cor 9:8).

EIGHT

Miracle Power at Your Fingertips

> *Words are powerful things. I once heard a stand-up comic lament: "Only a few words mumbled in church and you're married. Another few words mumbled in your sleep and you're divorced!"*

Proverbs tell us: "A word fitly spoken is like apples of gold in settings of silver" (Prv 25:11). For better or worse, words have a powerful effect on us all. Psychologists claim that even a single word can release compelling power. "Sale" is a word that will fill a store. Shouting "fire!" will empty it.

St. Augustine was converted by the power of a single sentence from the epistle to the Romans (see Romans 13:13-14). Olympic champion Willye White read Jesus' simple promise of peace (see John 14:27), which calmed her pre-competition tension so much that she went on to win the women's long jump (affirming yet again that "a Bible that's falling apart belongs to someone who isn't.")

Exemplifying God's typically direct approach to life's problems is Jesus' prompting for us to use his sacred Word to release miracle power: "If you remain in me, and *my word remains in you*, ask whatever you wish and it will be given you" (Jn 15:7).

This often overlooked but portentous statement is like a misplaced key to a seldom accessed roomful of miracles. "Ask whatever you wish" is a serendipitous offer to solve every type of problem—those related to marriage and family, health, finances, addictions, spiritual need, or whatever. Sounds like the stuff of pipe-dreams, doesn't it?

Unfortunately, this miraculous potential is seldom actualized. In spite of today's renewed interest in Scripture reading and study, the enormous power of God's Word goes largely neglected and hidden for most Christians. The mountain-moving dynamite is in place, but there is no detonator. That detonator is the double condition laid down in Jesus' promise: that we abide in the Lord and that his word abide in us.

Speaking to an interdenominational audience in 1979, Pope John Paul II stated that "the first priority of Christians today should be the preaching and living of God's word in all its purity and integrity, with all its exigencies and all its *power.*" In a 1982 allocution he again spoke of the power of God's word to contravene the "god of this age," the evil spirit that seeks to blind us to the light of the gospel (2 Cor 4:3).

The pontiff warned that "the world may accuse us of intransigence or irrelevance, but our criterion must always be fidelity to God's word in all its fullness and *power.*" He then added a tender word of persuasion: "Jesus himself gently challenges us, saying, in effect, 'trust my word; trust the *power* of my word to attract hearts, to convince consciences, to dissipate doubts, to soothe pain, to destroy falsehood and to insure authentic Christian freedom.'"

How can we fulfill Jesus' mandate to have his Word remain in us to release its powerful effects? Many Christians before us have given this question careful thought—the Greek and Latin Fathers of the Church, for example, and other great champions of the Word through the ages. An overview of their thinking indicates three elements which we must have if God's Word is to abide powerfully in us: first, an intense attraction, a *hunger,* for God's Word; second, a certain *knowledge* or familiarity with it; and third, a prayerful *devotion* in the use of that Word. All three elements work in concert, but it may be helpful to analyze each of them separately.

HUNGER FOR GOD'S WORD

Experienced drinkers say that sampling Scotch whiskey only occasionally won't give you a refined taste for it. Neither will merely perusing Scripture occasionally give you a taste for God's Word, much less a hunger. Hungering for God's Word implies being "consumed with a longing" for it, like the psalmist (Ps 119:20), or "treasuring his words more than daily bread," like Job (Jb 23:12).

Hungering for God's Word leads to "eating" it—not literally, of course (although the Old Testament prophets Ezekiel and Jeremiah did exactly this, as did John in the book of Revelation: see Ezekiel 3:1-3; Jeremiah 15:16; Revelation 10:9-10), but by devouring it with our minds and hearts. The effects of spiritually eating, digesting, and assimilating the Word are reflected in John Flavel's observation: "Only by devouring the Scriptures can one discover the best way of living, the noblest way of suffering, and the most comfortable way of dying."[1]

Do *you* hunger for God's word? Or do you simply admire it from a distance? Clever TV commercials for food can be quite entertaining, even for people who aren't hungry. Artistically displayed buffets can be admired even by those who have no appetite. Likewise, God's Word can be appreciated by some who do not really hunger for it. But the Bible is not simply to be admired from afar. It should be to us what the star was to the wise men. If we merely gaze at it, observe it, and admire its splendor without being led to Christ by it, its very purpose will be vitiated.

To calibrate your hunger for God's Word, try this test: If you were positive that you would *never* be able to obtain another Bible, how much would you sell yours for? Ten dollars? A million? Ten million? Would you clutch it as desperately as a starving person would clutch the last morsel of bread he needed to keep him alive? The intensity of your hunger for Scripture will reflect to a great extent the *power* you derive from it to solve your daily problems.

FAMILIARITY WITH GOD'S WORD

The second power trigger, familiarity with Scripture, implies a kind of knowledge that is unsatisfied with a shallow inquiry. A superficial investigation into God's Word will not only lead to distorted conclusions, as Peter reminds us (2 Pt 3:16), but also will fall short of providing insights needed to release the problem-solving power of the Word.

Jesus specifically highlighted the coupling of Scripture knowledge with Scripture power when he fulminated in response to the Sadducees, "You do not *know* the Scriptures or the *power* of God" (Mt 22:29). When it comes to God's Word, ignorance is impotence.

This kind of familiarity with the Bible does not require us to be Scripture scholars. It simply presumes that we are involved in an ongoing investigation of its meaning by frequently delving into it with wholesome inquisitiveness. A love letter is not read casually but with intense interest; it is read repeatedly, each phrase pondered for deeper meanings and connotations that might give more intimate insights into the very person of the beloved. No less assiduousness should be employed to God's "love letter," for in it he reveals himself. St. Jerome, who gave us the Latin Vulgate translation of the Bible, said that "ignorance of God's Word is ignorance of the Word made flesh."

Unfortunately, many people remain ignorant of God's Word, treating it more with indifference than disrespect. Even many Christians who expect society to respect the Bible neglect it themselves. According to a recent Barna Research Group survey, although 93 percent of Americans own a Bible, *half* say they never read it—including 23 percent of those identifying themselves as born-again Christians![2] Why, if all unused Bibles were dusted off simultaneously, we'd probably suffer a major dust storm.

A dusty Bible is as disgraceful for a Christian as was a rusty sword for a samurai warrior in Japan's feudal days. Scripture is, in fact, a weapon of divine power against the enemy—"the sword of the Spirit," Paul calls it (Eph 6:17). "A chapter a day keeps Satan away," the saying goes. But a dusty Bible is a sword in the scabbard and no threat to the enemy.

To put a new twist on an old metaphor, a Bible in the hand is worth two on the shelf. More to the point is the old aphorism, "A Bible known is worth a dozen merely owned." But, as some clever wordsmith has phrased it, "The Bible offers no loaves for the loafers." And so, although neglectful or lazy Christians do not usually regard themselves as spiritual loafers, some do come to recognize that they are spiritually undernourished.

This realization comes late for certain people; they begin to delve into the "Good Book," as they like to call it, when they become aware that eternity is just around the corner, in the sunset years of life. (I'm reminded of the elderly man who, when asked by his grandson why he read the Bible so much, responded, "I'm cramming for finals.")

"Nobody ever outgrows Scripture," claimed the great preacher Charles Spurgeon. "The book widens and deepens with our years." "The word of God will stand a thousand readings," adds James Hamilton, "and he who has gone over it most frequently is the surest of finding new wonders there."

Learned and unlearned alike can benefit from becoming familiar with God's love letter, for it is adaptable to each one's needs and talents. St. Gregory the Great suggested a unique metaphor: "Holy Scripture is a stream of running water," he said, "where an elephant may swim and a lamb may walk without losing its footing."

DEVOUT USE OF THE BIBLE

This brings us to the third prerequisite for releasing the power of God's Word, namely, devotion or prayerfulness in the use of Scripture. Even when one has hungered for the Word and attained some knowledge of it, apathy in devotion can abort its problem-solving power. Take another look at Jesus' promise in John 15:7; it requires not just that his Word abide in us, but also that we abide in him. This "branches in the vine" engrafting is necessary for the sap of grace to flow and for life-power to flourish.

Prayerfully abiding in the Lord as we immerse ourselves in his Word will widen the sluiceway of grace for multifarious uses of Scripture. We will see its power in prayer for deliverance and for healing, in private devotional prayer, in receiving the baptism in the Spirit, in exercising the charism of "holy persuasion," in reinforcing already accepted truth.

The grace received through Scripture will manifest itself with remarkable vigor in preaching, evangelizing, religious instruction of children, liturgy, counseling, private prayer, scriptural meditation, and in coping with countless workaday challenges, from patience-control to bereavement.

The power of Scripture will be clearly manifested in this way, however, only when God's Word is absorbed with a prayerful and incandescent love. Every Scripture scholar has a better-than-average familiarity with God's Word, but not every Scripture scholar is for that reason a paragon of holiness. Scholars with *devotional* attachment to God's Word experience its power far more than those who are fascinated with it merely *academically*. People who plod through the Bible more dutifully than fervently are often disappointed that it does not empower them to solve their problems, or even to cope with them. The reason, as Paul explains in 2 Corinthians 4:3, is a failure of faith in some of these readers or hearers of the Word; their minds are "veiled." Yet "whenever anyone *turns to the Lord,*" Paul also explains, "the veil is taken away" (2 Cor 3:16). To be empowered with the Word, we need a sincere, devout encounter with the Lord that leads to a new mind-set and God-permeated holiness (see Ephesians 4:23-24).

Scripture gives many examples of the results of such transformations. The grace-filled encounter with Jesus by the disciples on the Emmaus road empowered them in such a way that his words left their "hearts burning within them" (Lk 24:32). Acts 4:33 shows the apostles proclaiming the gospel message "with great *power*" because they had received that divine gift by which humans participate in God's own power: "grace was upon them." The lay evangelists from Cyprus and Cyrene converted vast crowds of people by the Word, "because the Lord's hand was with them" (Acts 11:21). As Paul later said of his own work, this was "a demonstration of the Spirit's *power*" (1 Cor 2:4); these evangelists planted the seed but knew that "God made it grow" by his power (3:6).

Paul repeatedly acknowledged that the "all-surpassing power" released in his own ministry was from God (2 Cor 4:7) and he even expressed amazement at it (see Romans 15:17-19). He recognized that his power to "do everything" came "through him who gives me strength" (Phil 4:13), and that he could receive it only because he was a branch engrafted on the vine.

Paul's prayer was that this power be replicated in all Christians:

I pray that... the Father may strengthen you with *power*,... that Christ may dwell in your hearts through faith.... that you... may have *power*... with all the saints... that you may be filled to the measure of all the fullness of God... who is able to do immeasurably more than all we ask or imagine, according to his *power* that is at work within us" (Eph 3:16-20).

And so, whether we receive the message or transmit it, that third empowering factor—a loving, close relationship with the Lord in his Word—is crucial, for it carries a supernal dynamism.

Combined with the other two requirements—hunger for the Word, and familiarity with it—it will ignite our hearts, like those of the disciples at Emmaus. And with our hearts "burning within us," we can set countless other hearts aflame in a conflagration of love.

NINE

Mary, "Our Tainted Nature's Solitary Boast"

A women's-lib speaker began her speech with a question: "Where would man be today if it were not for woman?" A disgruntled man at the back of the auditorium shouted out an unexpected answer to the question that was intended to be merely rhetorical: "He'd be back in the Garden of Eden, eating strawberries!" (Anything but apples, he figured.)

Did a woman cause all of society's problems? After all, it was Eve who committed the first sin, as Paul points out (see 1 Timothy 2:14). However, Paul also states that "sin entered the world through one man, and death through sin" (Rom 5:12). It was not that first sin, the sin of Eve, that caused our problems; it was the second sin, the sin of Adam, that contaminated the entire human race, including Eve herself. Paradoxically, the first sin was not the "original sin" (taken in its theological sense).

Eve's sin of disobedience downgraded her personal moral state. But in itself her sin did not infect her with a *proclivity* toward evil. Not so with Adam, whose sin did infect the entire human race, including Eve, with *a tendency* toward evil and with other weaknesses.

Eve incited Adam to sin without contaminating him, but Adam, by sinning, contaminated Eve. Though not the first sinner, he was the first human; he was thus the only person who by sin could contaminate all human beings—all his posterity—and deprive them of the primordial innocence they were intended to enjoy in their creational state of noncontamination. Adam could say to Eve, "Your counsel caused me to sin," but Eve could say to Adam, "Your sin caused me to lose my primordial innocence."

Thus, there were two kinds of failure in these two initial acts of disobedience to God's will. But by two later acts of obedience, this double disobedience would be counteracted and Satan defeated, as prophesied. "I will put enmity between you and the woman and between your offspring and hers," God told the serpent; "he will crush your head" (Gn 3:15).

Both acts of obedience occurred simultaneously, at the exact moment of the most extraordinary divine intervention in human history: the incarnation of God himself, an enfleshment of divinity in human form! One exalted act of obedience to the Father was carried out by the second Person of the Trinity. "The Word became flesh" (Jn 1:14) in order to save human beings. Only as the "new Adam" could he undergo the torturous redemptive act that was required to atone for the sins of Adam's human progeny (see Hebrews 2:14; Romans 3:25). By this, he recreated, as it were, a new kind of progeny: "As in Adam all die, so in Christ all will be made alive" (1 Cor 15:22).

At that same moment of the Incarnation, the other great act of obedience was performed by Mary, the "new Eve": "Be it done to me" (Lk 1:38). For this role Mary had been kept "full of grace." She was the *first sinless human being,* kept sinless by God's preserving grace to counterpoint the sin of Eve, the *first sinner*. In contrast to Eve's seduction of the first Adam, Mary consented to cooperate directly with the new Adam; she birthed him into the very world he would redeem, while aware that he was the only human ever born for the specific mission of dying.

The Incarnation and the Redemption—Nazareth and Calvary—are the "book-ends" or parentheses that demarcate the salvific solution to the pandemic of Adam's sin. Mary was intimately involved in both. Her total acquiescence to God's plan which began at the time of his enfleshment in her womb culminated on Calvary. On the cross Christ's obedience was expressed in his Passion, Mary's in her compassion as she "stood at the foot of the cross" (Jn 19:25). Just as Eve was co-active in the Fall without causing it, so the new Eve was co-active in the restoration (salvation) of humankind without causing it.

Moreover, Mary's joint activity with her Son was again demonstrated at Pentecost when his mystical body, the Church, was born. After all, a mother is always present at the birth of her offspring! Mary held a place of honor at that event (Acts 1:14). She therefore has a unique relationship with each and every one of us, actual or potential members of his now redeemed mystical body. Christ is the head of the body to which we have become joined, and God has extended Mary's relationship with her first-born child to us, his spiritual siblings: "He is the head of the body, the church; *he is the beginning and the firstborn*" (Col 1:18).

At Pentecost Mary's role as the new Eve culminated in her role as the new mother of all mankind. While not *causing* redemption, Mary was called by God to act jointly with her Son in reversing the universal damage of Adam's sin; she did this primarily by giving him a *physical body* through which he could suffer the atoning redemption.

Paul explains this mystery: "He [God] has reconciled you by Christ's *physical body* through death, to present you holy in his sight without blemish" (Col 1:22). Mary's maternal relationship to her Savior-Son in his physical body was paralleled, by God's design, in a maternal relationship with all of us in his redeemed mystical body. Why? Because in some way we, the saved, are all in him, the Savior: "We are members of his body" (Eph 5:30), and "in him all things hold together" (Col 1:17). This awesome and magnificent design of God for salvation history has lifted Mary to an utterly unique position among all humans.

REDISCOVERING "OUR BLESSED MOTHER"

An unfortunate fact about Mary's relationship to her Son's mystical body is this: While most Christians admire and respect Mary, they don't relate to her as our spiritual mother, which she is by virtue of our union with Jesus. Even though this union with Mary's Son is authenticated by Scripture, only a minority of Christians cultivate the spiritual and emotional intimacy with Mary that is implicitly mandated as a result.

Did you ever notice that awareness of this Marian relationship is found only among those with deep Marian devotion? They are the *only* ones who refer to Mary as "Our Mother." Others who simply admire and respect her refer to her as "the Virgin Mary"; they feel awkward calling her "mother"—except as Jesus' mother. As members of Christ's body, however, our relationship with Mary should involve more than mere admiration and respect; it should reflect the warm and loving spiritual intimacy that characterizes any wholesome mother-child relationship.

Another indicator of our awareness regarding Mary's relationship to us as members of her Son's mystical body: Do we refer to her as *"Blessed* Mother"? Only those who with a deep awareness of the scriptural implications of this truth, those who appreciate her as God's masterpiece, refer to Mary in this way. In calling her "blessed" they imitate the angel Gabriel and Elizabeth (Lk 1:28, 42). These Christians are in the minority, but they alone fulfill the biblical prophecy: "All generations will call me *blessed"* (Lk 1:48).

Even rarer than the use of that scriptural word, "blessed," in referring to Mary is the use of the word "our." Calling Mary the "Blessed Mother" says much about our love for her; calling her *"Our* Blessed Mother" bespeaks an added devotional element, which is similar to the effect of using the plural pronoun in the "Our Father." The "our" implies that we are clustered together, as it were, under the maternal mantle of "Our Blessed Mother." When any group becomes aware that all its members share in Mary's maternal love, they find it delightful to converse and discourse about her together as a community or assembly. Although all liturgical celebrations are, by nature, communitarian, Marian liturgical celebrations provide special occasion for joyous praise to God for "our tainted nature's solitary boast." Publicly, "her children arise and call her blessed" (Prv 31:28).

This nurtures a thriving devotion to Mary that fosters faith in her prayer before the Lord for our needs. Just as her intercession at Cana persuaded Jesus to work his first public miracle *for an assembly,* she intercedes for our needs today.

One final result of our membership in the mystical body of Mary's Son: we are all united in God's all-embracing redemptive love. God certainly loves us individually but he also loves us corporately, as Christ's body, the Church. Thus hugged t*ogether* in the divine embrace, we should network that love to each other. As John explains in a heartwarming exhortation: "God sent his Son as an atoning sacrifice for our sins. Dear friends, since God so loved us, we also ought to love one another.... If we love one another, God lives in us and his love is made complete in us" (1 Jn 4:10-12). John highlights the communitarian dimension of our growth in spiritual maturity, reminding us of an often overlooked theological principle: to have God's *saving love* "made complete" in us, we must allow it to manifest itself in us as a *sanctifying love.*

In this, Mary is our example and encouragement. Charity is called the queen of virtues, and it is in charity that our virtuous Queen excelled, by her incandescent love for God in her fellow humans, her children one and all. Reminding us of God's magnanimous love for each of us, she urges her children to let his divine love be made complete in us by our love for one another in Jesus.

Mary's pleading for her children to love one another is a

dominant theme in her many reported apparitions through the centuries. Thus she urges the members of her Son's body to cultivate charity, the virtue that God's Word places above all others as the capstone of holiness: "Over all these virtues put on love, *which binds all together in perfect unity"* (Col 3:14).

IMITATION—THE HIGHEST FORM OF COMPLIMENT

Corresponding to Mary's God-planned uniqueness by reason of her co-activity in God's redemptive plan is her equally God-planned uniqueness in holiness. She is one of a kind, both in her "positive" spirituality (her virtue) and in her "negative" spirituality (her sinlessness). Conceived without having been infected by Adam's sin, she was preserved "full of grace" throughout her life. Because of these prerogatives, Mary is indeed "our tainted nature's solitary boast," as the poet William Wordsworth wrote in his sonnet, "The Virgin." Extolled through the centuries as a paradigm of holiness, Mary is the perfect example of how human creatures might relate to their Creator, in absolute conformity to the plan and will of God.

The Second Vatican Council gives us three purposes for practicing devotion toward Mary or any saint: to imitate the good example of their life; to enjoy holy, loving fellowship in the "communion of saints," that blessed interfacing of believers in heaven and on earth; and to ask for their intercessory prayer to God for our needs of body, mind, and spirit.[1] In our relationship with Mary, the first of these three purposes should be our top priority: imitating her virtues as we strive for holiness in our walk with the Lord.

There are fifty-six virtues in the "catalogue of virtues"—some two-hundred if all of their subdivisions are included. Mary's soul was bedecked with all virtues to a supereminent degree—a veritable spiritual smorgasbord to choose from for imitation. As I make this observation, I can almost hear the obvious objection erupting: The Bible doesn't command us to imitate Mary or any saint, but only Jesus. It was Jesus, not Mary, who said, "Learn of me...."

This objection is quite valid in some ways; the very meaning of Christian life is indeed the imitation of Christ and the realization of his life in us (see Ephesians 5:1-2). However, Mary has a special place in this scheme of things—one far superior to other saints. She was able to imitate God's virtues better than anyone else; in her, Christ's grace was realized most perfectly, by her Immaculate Conception.[2]

While Jesus is the perfect Redeemer, Mary is the one most perfectly redeemed, for God prevented sin from ever touching her life rather than merely removing it. *She was not saved from sin but saved from sinning.* To have this privilege Mary needed salvation, and she was truly saved. This is why she said "I rejoice in God my *Savior*" (Lk 1:46). She appreciated her salvation more than any other human creature.

Therefore, among all the saved, Mary is the best Christ-imitator. So our striving to imitate Mary both in her Christlike virtues and in her Christlike sinlessness does not in any way detract from our imitation of Jesus. It actually reaffirms it, but from another perspective—a perspective relative to God's most godly creature, who like us depended on him for salvation.

Paul himself had no qualms about telling his followers to imitate his own example. To the Corinthians and other Christian communities, he explained the principle that underlay his proposal: "Follow my example, as I follow the example of Christ" (1 Cor 11:1; 4:16; see also 1 Thessalonians 1:6; 2:14; 2 Thessalonians 3:9; Philippians 3:17; Hebrews 6:12; 13:9; 1 Timothy 1:16; 1 Peter 3:13). In other words, he asked them to imitate himself, but only to the extent that his behavior imitated that of Jesus.

There is another response to those who would imitate no one but Christ. In the spectrum of Christ's majestic splendor, there are areas that cannot be imitated—for instance, his role in creation, his status as founder of the Church and head of the mystical body, and his redemptive love. But Mary provides a model of virtue that is not totally beyond our imitation. Even her sinlessness we can *strive* to imitate.

If you want to choose any one of Mary's virtues to imitate, I suggest starting with the one that is found at the very fountain-head of her coredemptive role, namely, obedience to God's will. Mary's overall response was one of perfect *conformity* with God's will. By her "vocational" conformity she provided fallen humanity with a Redeemer to heal the contaminating effects of *nonconformity* with God's will (Adam's sin of disobedience.) Beyond that, Mary's interior and exterior life was a lived-out conformity to God's will that makes her the supreme example of the mind-boggling effects of total abandonment to God: "Those who *obey* his commands live in him and he in them" (1 Jn 3:24).

CULTIVATING MARIAN DEVOTION

In order to *venerate* Mary (it would be sacrilegious to *worship* her or any creature!), we must relate to her as a living, loving person—a pre-eminently special person who is also our spiritual mother and who loves us personally with an indescribable love. This personal relationship with Mary requires a *special* grace from God. If he hasn't bestowed that grace on you, plead for him to do so. If he has, then thank him for it passionately.

Many non-Catholics and even many marginal Catholics are not disposed to seek a personal relationship with Mary because they were not acculturated to Marian devotion from early childhood. Like countless other good or bad human attitudes and habits—family affection, love of classical music, habits of gambling, attitudes about divorce, use of drugs and alcohol, and so on—Marian devotion is "more caught than taught."

Culture really does play a major role in religion and spirituality. Just try identifying with a devout Muslim at prayer, or a Jew at the Wailing Wall, or a Hindu at a crematory funeral. Likewise, if you try to explain what goes on at Marian shrines to someone who is not devoted to Mary—to describe the awesome interior love-surges or the exterior phenomena—you would usually get a disappointing response.

A deep and abiding awareness of Mary as our spiritual mother is one of the most beautiful, comforting, and spiritually uplifting insights that can be given by the Holy Spirit. It is an insight that involves the kind of "spiritual wisdom and understanding" that Paul prayed would be given to the Colossians and Ephesians (Col 1:9; Eph 5:17). And since all *authentic* Marian devotion points to Christ, as Vatican II proclaimed[3], all true Marian devotees have a much richer devotion to Jesus because of it.

One of the greatest rewards of filial devotion and love to Mary, this side of heaven, is the incalculable *joy* it engenders. There is a joy in honoring our heavenly Father, the divine Artisan, for fashioning Mary, his creative masterwork; joy in being, in some way, another Jesus for Mary; joy in feeling constantly secure and at peace because we trust in her protective love and enjoy her maternal solicitude; joy in experiencing success by her blessing on all of our works done for God's glory, as she teaches us to rely on her divine Son. There is the joy of making Mary known, loved, and served; the joy of seeing her honored both by God who "has done great things" for her and by humans—"all generations will call me blessed" (Lk 1:49, 48); the joy of growing in love for Jesus under her tutelage; the joy of bringing happiness to Jesus by honoring Mary, and happiness to Mary by honoring Jesus.

The saintly Marianist Brother Leonard once wrote: "To give Jesus the delightful joy of loving Mary on earth through me, and to give Mary the joy of seeing her Son live again in me—what a glorious thought!" Is it rash to say that those lacking such joy are missing something great in their spiritual life?

Let us never weary of praising God, as Mary praised him, for all she has received from him for *us* to enjoy and admire. Truly, "the Mighty One has done great things" for *us* by doing such great things for Mary, "our tainted nature's solitary boast."

While we are here on earth, we can be a part of the generations who call her blessed and admire God's magnificent masterpiece. And when we actually see Mary in heaven, our honor and admiration will be like an endlessly sustained peak experience. To a major extent Mary will be the reason for our joy as we revel in the goodness of God who fashioned this greatest wonder of his splendorous creation.

TEN

Get to Know Your Guardian Angel

Dear Father Hampsch: Do I really have a guardian angel who is with me constantly, or is that just a pious belief that is taught to young children? If I could be certain that I have my own personal guardian angel with me constantly, the implications for me would be enormous!

This insightful person was posing to me a question I've often heard before. Is it *reasonable* to believe in what you cannot see? Absolutely!

You can't see air, and yet you wouldn't doubt that it is essential for your very life. You can't see electricity, and yet today, your life would be unthinkable without it. You can't see atoms, and yet without them your very body—and even the entire cosmos—would not exist. You can't see heat, magnetism, gravity, cosmic radiation or any kind of radiant energy, yet without them you couldn't survive. Many of the "invisible" material things around us are some of the most significant entities in God's creation, in assuring our well-being and even our very existence.

Along with invisible material realities, God has provided us also with invisible spiritual realities, such as virtue, actual and sanctifying grace, and even his own divine presence in many forms, from cosmic to Eucharistic. Among these invisible spiritual realities are those super-intelligent, super-powerful entities called angels, including those holy angelic beings custom-assigned to our personal care as our constant companions, called guardian angels.

Can it really be true that each of us has an angelic companion constantly with us, who is at the same time enjoying the ineffable bliss of the Beatific Vision—seeing the very face of God while in our presence? Is the teaching about guardian angels just a pious belief taught to young children and rhapsodized by a saccharine poem, "Angel of God, my guardian dear..."? If we could *really* believe that each of us has such a personal, loving, God-assigned companion living with us at every moment of our lives, this belief would impact our behavior and attitudes in ways that would be positively staggering and radically life-changing.

Yes, each of us does indeed have a personal guardian angel and as my correspondent realized, acknowledging and understanding this truth would utterly transform any person's life, just as the many angelic apparitions mentioned in the Bible transformed the lives of those who saw them.

Just think about what it might mean to truly know, either by faith or by actually having seen an angel, that each one of us has the awesome privilege of a personally assigned spiritual guardian. Why, the most forlorn widow in the world would no longer languish in loneliness or self-pity. Those tempted to lust would find it unthinkable to sin in the presence of their heavenly companion. The discouraged or despairing would be reinvigorated by the radiant presence of their angel companion. And how could anyone ever again think there is such a thing as solitary confinement?

Scripture refers to angels often—more than three-hundred times. They usually appear as "ministering spirits sent to serve" (Heb 1:14), and their primary ministerial role is acting as messengers. In fact, the Greek word for angel, *angelos*, means messenger. The guardian angels who are assigned to us individually seem to have the main function of guarding and protecting us: "He will command his angels... to *guard* you in all your ways..." (Ps 91:11).

There is a class of evil spirits (fallen angels) known as "familiar spirits" (these are referred to in several places in the Old Testament). They are called "familiar" because they become closely acquainted with our weaknesses so as to attack us in those areas. Our guardian angels, too, become familiar with our weaknesses and strengths, but they are commissioned by God to protect, inspire, encourage, support, and pray for us.

The teaching about the existence of personal *guardian* angels (as distinguished from teachings about angels in general) is a doctrine of the Church that is classed as *proxima fidei:* a consistent and scripturally supported teaching that is not formally defined as dogma. The existence of guardian angels is affirmed by theological luminaries like St. Jerome and St. Thomas Aquinas, whose extensive writings on angels earned him the title "Angelic Doctor."

The most direct scriptural reference to such personally assigned angels is found in Jesus' words in Matthew 18:10, which are sandwiched between his remarks about childlike humility (perceiving one's own helplessness) and the helplessness of a straying sheep needing rescue: "See that you do not look down on any one of these little ones. For I tell you that their angels in heaven always see the face of my Father in heaven."

Help for the helpless is provided by personally assigned angels, as Jesus indicates. Exemplified by the child that Jesus called into his presence, the helpless, lowly, or weak (children or adults) are called "little ones." In God's eyes, though, they are not little but great (Mt 18:4), and their greatness or nobility is highlighted by their being assigned personal angels who are constantly enraptured by the vision of God himself. Jesus' words—"any one of these" and "their angels"—indicate that these protectors are not assigned merely as overseers of groups but of individuals, that is, as personal guardian angels. Accordingly, the early Christians often spoke of an angel as being "his" or "her" angel (see Acts 12:15).

The Old Testament, too, presents angelic protection as extended not only to groups (see Exodus 23:20; Daniel 12:1; 2 Maccabees 11:6) but also to individuals (see Daniel 6:22). (Eventually, some Jewish rabbis also came to teach that every individual has a personal guardian angel.) The psalmist acknowledged some personalism in angelic protection, at least for himself, and hinted at it for everyone: "Those who plot my ruin... the angel of the Lord drives them away" (Ps 35:4-5); "This poor man called, and the Lord heard him.... The angel of the Lord encamps around [each of] those who fear him, and he delivers them" (Ps 34:6-7); and the passage that Satan quoted when he tempted Jesus, "He will command his angels concerning you to guard you in all your ways" (Ps 91:11; Mt 4:6).

These passages show guarding as a one-to-one function of the angels. Others present the angels' role of guiding: Abraham's servant is led to find just the right wife for his master's son (see Genesis 24:7); Hagar is given direction (see Genesis 16:7); Tobias is guided by the archangel Raphael (see Tobit 5:4) on a journey that leads to marriage and healing. Angels perform rescue operations (see Daniel 6:22; Acts 5:19; 12:7-11). They also provide encouragement in critical situations, as in the case of Paul just before he was shipwrecked (see Acts 27:23).

Most of us have not had angelic apparitions like these. Our appreciation of the privilege of having a guardian angel comes from faith more often than from experience. Yet countless people have experienced miraculous protection by their guardian angel. Many have been helped by persons they suspected of being angels in disguise—a possibility mentioned in Hebrews 13:2.

Does everyone have a guardian angel, or is it only the righteous who enjoy this protection? The question is debatable. St. Jerome and St. Basil held that serious sin drives away one's guardian angel, leaving sinners vulnerable to spiritual and perhaps even physical hurt in life's spiritual warfare. Although this is somewhat conjectural (and perhaps contrary to Jesus' remarks about God's indiscriminate beneficence to saint and sinner alike: see Matthew 5:45), there may be some basis for this view. God does withdraw many favors from those who disobey him (see Deuteronomy 28:15-68).

Psalm 91:9 promises angelic protection "*if* you make the Most High your dwelling." Psalm 34:7 says that "the angel of the Lord encamps around *those who fear* [reverence] *him*." And Hebrews 1:14 clearly states that angels are "sent to serve those who will inherit salvation." Although it is possible that God may send angels to protect those who will not inherit salvation, there is no scriptural indication that he does so.

Doesn't it seem unthinkable, perhaps even culpable, to ignore or neglect such an awesome, personalized gift from God? Just think for a moment of who these guardians are: part of God's myriads of angels, "mighty ones who do his bidding" (Ps 103:20), beings with a superlative intellect and incredible power. Of the nine angelic "choirs," or orders, referred to in various places in Scripture, our guardians belong to the order closest to the human level. As angels, they are lower than archangels, virtues, powers, principalities, dominations, thrones, cherubim, and seraphim. Yet their abilities and intelligence and holiness are inconceivably greater than ours. Having such an angelic companion is better than having a super-holy Superman as our private intercessor, servant, advisor, bodyguard, and friend!

How important, then, to cultivate devotion to our guardian angels. One helpful way of doing this, I have found, is to meditate on the personal aspect of God's promise in Psalm 91:11 (and surrounding verses): "He will command his angels concerning *you* to guard *you* in all *your* ways." By sending you such a customized gift, God is showing personal interest in *you* as an individual. He has selected a delegate to guard you "in all your ways"—in your ups and downs, in your waking and sleeping hours, when you're alone or with others, in your joys and in your sufferings, in your successes and your failures. No wonder St. Francis de Sales urges, "Make yourself familiar with angels and behold them frequently in spirit; for without being seen, they are present with you."

Your appreciation of your guardian angel will reach its scintillating climax at your death. Then your guardian will take you by the hand to lead you to the arms of God while, as Shakespeare phrased it in *Hamlet*, "flights of angels sing thee to thy rest." And as your close personal friend who has known you better than anyone, your angel will rejoice along with you for all eternity in the ineffable bliss of the vision of God.

Truly, those who believe this doctrine of guardian angels with all their heart are utterly transformed in time and for all eternity!

ELEVEN

Joy, the Sparkle of Life

> *In a dignified church worship of "God's frozen people" an exuberant lady shouted, "Praise the Lord!"*
>
> *An usher tried to quell her enthusiasm. "You can't have outbursts like that in this church," he protested.*
>
> *"I can't suppress my joy since I found the Lord!" the woman explained.*
>
> *"If you found the Lord," stated the usher, "you didn't find him here."*

When I heard this rib-tickling story, I couldn't help but think of the words of Isaiah 49:13: "Shout for joy... rejoice O earth... for the Lord comforts his people." The story even made the words of Jesus take on new meaning for me, "No one will take away your joy" (Jn 16:22). Only for those who have truly "found the Lord" can there be true, lasting spiritual joy, as distinguished from worldly joy or mirth. Spiritual joy is like the Bethlehem star, worldly joy like a passing meteor. The former is like a floodlight, the latter like a quick-burning match flame.

The French writer Leon Bloy expressed a maxim when he observed: "Spiritual joy is an infallible sign of the presence of the Holy Spirit in the soul." This is logical, since it is an out-cropping of the first fruit of the Spirit, love (see Galatians 5:22). Joy is love exulting, someone has said. And where true love exists, so does true joy. Peter refers to this combination: "You love him, even though you do not see him... and are filled with inexpressible and glorious joy" (1 Pt 1:8). John repeats Jesus' promise about the effects of loving him: "Abide in my *love,* so that my *joy* may be in you" (Jn 15:10). Indeed, how could any-one be joyless while experiencing this mutual union with God?

The Greek word for joy that is used in the New Testament is *chara;* it can connote cheerfulness, gladness, exuberance or overflow, or calm delight. It appears sixty times in the New Testament alone, while the word for "rejoice" appears seventy-two times. The frequency of these words in Scripture suggests the importance of joy as a fruit of the Spirit. But why be joyful?

The first reason for joy relates to salvation or to the Savior who effects it, since salvation is the culminating joyful event of all human history. This is why the news of the Savior's birth was announced as "tidings of great joy" (Lk 2:10). This is why the Magi, "when they saw the star, were overjoyed" (Mt 2:10). This is why Mary proclaimed in her canticle, "My soul magnifies the Lord and my spirit rejoices in God my Savior" (Lk 1:47); she was celebrating the Savior's arrival and anticipating the great sal-vation event. And even before Mary we see this salvation-joy sparkling in the scriptural forerunners of her Magnificat—in the prayers of Hannah: "My heart rejoices in the Lord" (1 Sm 2:1); in Isaiah: "I delight greatly in the Lord; my soul rejoices in my God, for he has clothed me in the garments of salvation" (Is 61:10); and Habakkuk: "I will rejoice in the Lord, I will be joy-ful in God my Savior" (Hb 3:18).

Salvation is the receiving end of redemption and essentially, redemption means rescuing. Jesus, our rescuing Redeemer, claimed the prophecy of Isaiah: "The Spirit of the Lord... has sent me... to release the oppressed" (Lk 4:18-19). It was this joyful release from bondage that the eunuch experienced, "rejoicing" after his baptism by Philip (Acts 8:39); likewise, the

Samaritan city where Philip proclaimed the salvation message resounded with "great joy" (8:8). Paul too spoke of salvation joy in God through Jesus (for example, see Romans 5:11). The release of hostages is always an occasion of rejoicing, as many a newscast has shown. How much greater should be our joy over our salvation-release from the bonds of sin and darkness!

A second reason for joy: we look forward to the fullness of salvation—"an inheritance... kept in heaven for you... until the coming of the salvation that is ready to be revealed in the last time. In this you greatly rejoice" (1 Pt 1:4-6). Anticipatory joy might be compared to the hopes of a child on Christmas Eve. Unlike our fleeting earthly joys, however, the joy that looks ahead to heaven is based on "a hope that does not disappoint us" (Rom 5:5).

A third reason for joy—and this one is related to anticipatory joy—is that our sufferings are not meaningless. Therefore, while "joy in the midst of suffering" may be an oxymoron, it is not a contradiction.

Peter reassures us that "though now for a little while you may have had to suffer grief in all kinds of trials... you are filled with inexpressible and glorious joy, for you are receiving the goal of your faith, the salvation of your souls" (1 Pt 1:6-9). After much physical suffering, Paul and Barnabas reminded the Pisidians that "we must go through many hardships to enter the Kingdom of God" (Acts 14:22). It was with this ultimate hope in mind that Paul could say "we rejoice in our sufferings" (Rom 5:3).

Joy in suffering is not morbid masochism, which is a psychopathological state. And to note a more subtle distinction, joy is not the same as happiness, although both are desirable. Happiness has to do with "happenings" or "happenstance"; it is a pleasant emotional response of gaiety to a pleasant situation or happening and is therefore incompatible with sorrowful or painful situations.

True joy, on the other hand, can be present in suffering and is much more than a surface emotion. It is a fruit of the Spirit—

a deep, positive spiritual exultation; a profound, jubilant inner response of delight to the presence of God's Spirit within; a rejoicing in his loving providence that always works for good in guiding all of life's events, whether pleasant or painful. As Richard Wagner wrote, "Joy is not in things; it is in us."

While happiness does not require faith, joy as a fruit of the Spirit does, especially when sufferings are involved. How much easier it would be to endure them if Jesus were to appear and tell us what he told the apostles: "in this world you will have trouble. But take heart [cheer up—rejoice]! I have overcome the world" (Jn 16:33).

Those with deep faith may not need such an apparition or personal revelation to believe this. But most of us can recognize and admit to a faith-weakness that should prompt us to pray with the apostles, "Increase our faith!" (Lk 17:5). We can also remember and take heart from the Lord's words to the church in Smyrna, which apply to us too: "Do not be afraid of what you are about to suffer.... Be faithful (full of faith throughout the trial), even to the point of death, and I will give you the crown of life" (Rv 2:10).

Thus the "faith-full" soul finds a twofold joy in suffering. First, there is joy in recognizing that all suffering is not just a hardship to be stoically accepted but is a part of God's loving providence by which Christ shares his cross with us. Second, suffering results in a joyful hundredfold reward that "does not disappoint" (Rom 5:5). Peter links both these reasons for joy in suffering in one sentence: "Rejoice that you participate in the sufferings of Christ, so that you may be overjoyed when his glory is revealed" (1 Pt 4:13).

Of course, learning to live in the light of these truths day by day is a long hard process. This is why these words of James are some of the most challenging in Scripture: "Consider it pure joy whenever you face trials of many kinds, because you know that the testing of your faith develops perseverance. Perseverance must finish its work so that you may be mature and complete, not lacking anything" (Jas 1:2-4). James is saying that our spiritual maturity is calibrated by the degree to which we experience "pure joy" in our trials. Stop for a moment and consider his words in the light of your present suffering, whether it be physical, emotional, spiritual, interpersonal.

Most of us recognize that we still have a way to go along this arduous road to pure joy. But there are many who show us that it can be done. I once knew a lady who was severely crippled with arthritis and covered head-to-foot with psoriasis. She spent twenty-eight years in a squalid fifty-bed ward in Cook County Hospital in Chicago (a record for any patient in the hospital's history), with never a complaint in all that time, as the nurses told me just before she died. Yet this woman's joy was deep, for she spent her years of torturous agony in the loving presence of God, offering up the sacrifice of what she had loved to do best—and had done with masterful skill: playing the organ and the piano.

Shortly before her death I questioned this woman about joy in suffering. Her reply was a touching masterpiece of spiritual insight into the loving providence of God that operates in and through trials. She told me that her joy was further enhanced by her offering all her suffering for me, that I might become an effective priest to bring many souls to the Lord. She died on Christmas Day and was buried in a pauper's grave; only four people attended her funeral—not even a sufficient number for pallbearers.

To all appearances this woman's life was a dismal failure, but I was privileged to see it for what it really was—a monumental success. Even now I feel the effects of her deathbed promise that she would pray for me in heaven every time I stepped into the pulpit to preach God's word. Her place in heaven may well be higher than that of many who enjoyed places of honor and reputations for holiness in this life.

If this woman's joy on earth was so great in the midst of such agony, what must her joy in heaven be now? Perhaps Psalm 149:4-9 best describes her status: "The Lord takes delight in his people; he crowns the humble with salvation. Let the saints rejoice in this honor and sing for joy on their beds.... The praise of God is in their mouths... this is the glory of all his saints."

Perhaps you have traveled from a point of seeing only misery in your cross to one where you can see at least some joy in it. If so, you might ask yourself how close this is to the "pure joy" James mentions. Is it perhaps a joy polluted with tinges of resentment or with doubt about God's love and concern for you? Is it a joy adulterated with self-pity? Does it seek a reason for the suffering with questions like, "Why me?" or "Why this type of suffering?"—why not depression rather than arthritis, or a phobia instead of the misery of an unhappy marriage or divorce?" If our joy in suffering is really pure joy, it is undiluted with such limitations.

We are called to move beyond the less than mature level of spirituality that most of us Christians operate in—what I call the kindergarten or elementary school level of faith—to joy that is complete even amid trials. Austerities and persecution notwithstanding, John the Baptist could yet claim that his joy was complete (see John 3:29). This *complete* joy is available to each of us too, for Jesus said, "Ask and you will receive, and your joy will be complete" (Jn 16:24). Remember too—and be heartened—that the same Jesus who was "sorrowful unto death" in the garden of Gethsemane also prayed for us, his followers, "that my joy may be in you and that your joy may be complete" (Jn 15:11). He further prayed that we might "have the completeness of my joy within them" (Jn 17:13).

Paul also prayed for his disciples to have this complete joy: "May the God of hope fill you with *all* joy," he told the members of the church in Rome (Rom 15:13). Prayers like this must have been realized in many of the Jewish and Gentile Christians in Asia Minor, for Peter wrote to some of them that in spite of "suffering grief in all kinds of trials... you are filled with inexpressible and glorious joy" (1 Pt 1:6-8). This certainly sounds like the complete or pure joy that James urges—unadulterated with self-pity or any other pollutants.

Of course, Paul himself is a model of complete joy. Even

while chained in a prison at Philippi, he could write, "I will continue to rejoice, for I know that... through the help given by the Spirit of Jesus Christ, what has happened to me will turn out for my deliverance" (Phil 1:19). This unflagging continuity of joy in spite of any hardships is a sign of the fruit of the Spirit of Jesus, as Paul acknowledges. He urges the Philippians also to "rejoice in the Lord"—a God-focus that assures an unwavering continuity which Paul expresses by the word "always": "Rejoice in the Lord always. I will say it again: Rejoice!" (Phil 4:4). Christ's indwelling Spirit is the source or "headwater" of the river of joy that flows with a continuity, unperturbed by any adversity.

The author of Hebrews holds before us the perfect model of complete joy in suffering: Jesus, the "perfecter of our faith, who for the *joy* set before him endured the cross.... Consider him... so that you will not grow weary and lose heart" (Heb 12:2-3). Jesus himself told us not to lose heart, for he has overcome the world. (Jn 16:33). When we receive this great fruit of Jesus' Spirit as the first outcropping of love, we become able to receive the truth of such statements—and also to make sense of certain paradoxes: "You will have trouble," Jesus says, but "do not let your hearts be troubled" (Jn 16:33; 14:1).

How can this pure and complete joy be activated in you? Abide in the love of Jesus (see John 15:10-11) through daily, prayerful reading of God's love letter, the Bible, and through deep personal prayer alone with the Lord. "In his presence is the fullness of joy" (Ps 16:11), and an ongoing encounter with the Lord will result in ongoing joy, "like streams of water in the desert" (Is 32:2).

After their ecstatic encounter with the newborn Savior of the world, and still quivering from the angel's announcement of "tidings of great joy," the poor humble shepherds (looked down on as among the dregs of society in that day) joyfully returned to their flocks, "glorifying and praising God for all the things they had heard and seen" (Lk 2:20). A true encounter with Jesus, "the Joy of Israel," will transform anyone with a touch of heaven's joy—a sparkle of God's own divine ecstasy.

PART III

In God We Trust: Coping with Potholes, Pitfalls and Panic

A friend of mine was surprised at the extraordinary interest of his fellow office workers in the progress of his wife's pregnancy. Almost every day someone would inquire about her progress or about the doctor's reports, and especially about the expected arrival time. It wasn't until later that he discovered that a "betting pool" had been set up among his fellow employees, the winner being the one who guessed the day, hour, and minute closest to the moment of the anticipated birth. The buzz of interest, he soon recognized, was not so much the shared joy of the expected birth but the greedy desire to win the office bet.

False motives have a way of infiltrating both our social life and our spiritual life. The author of Proverbs scorns the hypocrisy of "the kind of man who is always thinking about the cost... his heart is not with you" (Prv 23:7). False or superficial motivation, like toxic waste, subtly poisons some Christians who seek to validate their Christianity by symbols rather than substance—bumper stickers, ostentatious use of religious jewelry, and Christian jargon.

What *really* validates our Christianity—especially in the maelstrom of adversity—is our character, which reveals itself in many interior goals and choices: our zeal for building the Lord's kingdom, our lifestyle decisions, our dedication to the pursuit of holiness, and our sensitivity to impediments to our union with God. Recognizing the dangers of hypocrisy and wrong motives, Paul sets the standard for living a truly Christian life: "Love must be sincere. Hate what is evil; cling to what is good... Keep your spiritual fervor, serving the Lord. Be joyful in hope, patient in affliction, faithful in prayer" (Rom 12:9-12). Those inspired words, full of concise and sound advice about dodging spiritual road hazards, epitomize the contents of this part of the book.

When we are confronted with potholes and pitfalls on our heaven-bound journey, when we are shocked by the realization of our own lassitude and character flaws, discouraged by apparent non-answers to prayer, or overwhelmed by adversities—it is then that we must, with unwavering faith, call upon the Lord, "who is able to keep you from falling and to present you before his glorious presence without fault and with great joy" (Jude 24). And that same faith will dissolve our panic and strengthen us with insuperable confidence, like Paul, to move forward on our trek—"to finish the race and complete the task the Lord has given" (Acts 20:24).

Let us strive to emulate the resilient, single-hearted, faith-activated trust of David, one of God's favorites. He knew how to confront potholes, pitfalls and panic: "In God I trust, I will not be afraid.... For you have delivered.... my feet from stumbling, that I may walk before God in the light of life" (Ps 56:11-13).

TWELVE

The Art of Suffering— Way to Grow

> *On school playgrounds across America the "report" is circulating that a new kind of headache relief is on the market—a pill made of aspirin and glue. It's for people with "splitting" headaches!*

Anyone who has suffered—and who hasn't?—has wished for a simple solution to the ever-present problem of pain, suffering, hardship, and tribulation that plagues all of us earthlings.

Since the fall of Adam and Eve, the "mystery of misery" has been much complained about but seldom explored in depth by the average person. But Christ unveiled much of that mystery by his teachings on suffering; he also affirmed it existentially by undergoing a life of suffering, capped by a torturous death. "He suffered death so that... he might taste death for everyone" (Heb 2:9). Identifying with us in our human anguish, he showed divine sympathy and taught the art of suffering by his example.

"In this world you will have trouble," Christ assured the disciples (Jn 16:33). Indeed, given the fact of original sin, life's hurts truly are inevitable. But what escapes most people is that these hardships can produce a response that is not bitter, but bittersweet. There is sweetness in suffering—but how few find it! Do you know many who follow Paul's injunction to "*rejoice* in sufferings" (Rom 5:3)? Many who can exclaim with him, "For the sake of Christ, I *delight* in weaknesses, in insults, in hardships, in persecutions, in difficulties" (2 Cor 12:10)? Many who consistently follow the urging of James: "Consider it *pure joy*, my brothers, whenever you face trials of many kinds" (Jas 1:2)? Paul's "delight" and James' "pure joy" in adversity are gratifications that faith-weak souls never taste.

Of course, it is not the suffering itself that we are told to rejoice in but rather the beneficial results of the suffering. God does not expect us to thrill at the news that a loved one has been stricken with cancer or that we have lost our job or that our child has Down Syndrome. "Give thanks *in* all circumstances," Paul tells us—not *for* all circumstances—"for this is God's will for you in Christ Jesus" (1 Thes 5:18). (In fact, God intends us to actively seek every means of alleviating such suffering; only when we have exhausted the possibilities should we "offer it up" with resigned—yet ever trusting—hearts.)

We are to rejoice and be thankful because we believe that God will work through such things for our ultimate good, even though that good is not immediately apparent. The only requirements are that we continue to love God and conform to his will and purpose (see Romans 8:28).

To greet every one of life's hurts with joy and thanks, with love for the God who sends or permits the adversity, and with gracious accommodation to his plan—this is the real art of suffering. And this is the example Jesus set for us. The author of Hebrews tells us to "fix our eyes on Jesus, the author and perfecter of our faith, who for the *joy* set before him endured the cross" (Heb 12:2). Thus, if we are to grow spiritually, we must look beyond our hurts to the joy that is ahead, in union with the perfecter of our faith.

The road of the cross is really a crossroad—a junction of

choice. We must turn either right or left, choose either to accept each cross or rebel against it. We all want to grow, of course, but we tend to resist the process of accepting the crosses required for growth. We focus on the hurtful events instead of using the eyes of faith to see the growth that God intends through them.

Jesus explained that a soul must be painfully pruned or cut back (the bitter part of suffering) in order for it to enjoy the sweet fruitfulness to which it is called. Only faith-hardy souls—branches that remain vitally linked to the Vine—submit to being cut back; faith-weak souls are cut off by the divine Gardener as fruitless branches (see John 15:1-4). This is the basic rationale for suffering, or pruning—*growth to the point of fruitfulness.* But how easy it is to lose sight of this truth when one is struggling with the crushing weight of one's cross!

SIX LEVELS OF FAITH IN SUFFERING

Our response to suffering provides a yardstick to measure our spiritual maturity. Which of these six groups do you relate to most easily?

1. *Those who believe in God* but resent him for allowing suffering, especially their own or a family member's.

2. *Those who have faith enough to pray for relief* but are resentful when God doesn't send that relief promptly.

3. *Those who passively tolerate the suffering,* not rebelling against God's will. They languish in their anguish, not using its benefits or seeing it as a gift of God.

4. *Those who actively rejoice in suffering* as a customized, growth-stimulating pruning, fully aware that "in all things God works for the good of those who love him" (Rom 8:28).

5. *Those who rejoice in the eternal reward that is theirs through patiently enduring malicious acts or persecution by others,* under God's permissive will. They find support in Jesus' words: "When people insult you, persecute you and falsely

say all kinds of evil against you... rejoice and be glad, because great is your reward in heaven" (Mt 5:11-12).

6. *Those who rejoice when they are victimized by human-caused suffering for an even higher motive*—the privilege of being united with Christ in his suffering. They are sustained by Peter's words: "Rejoice that you participate in the suffering of Christ, so that you may be overjoyed when his glory is revealed.... You are blessed, for the Spirit of glory and of God rests on you" (1 Pt 4:13-14).

This spectrum of suffering-tested faith reveals a wide range of responses, from faith-weak to faith-hardy. The greater the faith, the greater the insight into the value of suffering, and of course, the greater the reward. The three highest levels entail active *rejoicing* in the spiritual benefits of suffering. In the lower levels the tragedy is not the experience of suffering but the waste of suffering.

GROWING PAINS

The cecropia moth struggles mightily to emerge from its cocoon, but this effort is essential to its growth. Snipping open the cocoon to ease its struggle would leave the moth crawling helplessly with crimped and shriveled wings. A mother eagle lines her nest with thorns, jagged bones, and sharp stones, which are then covered with feathers, tufts of wool, and animal fur. To encourage her fledgling eaglets to try their wings for flight, she removes the fluffy topping and exposes the uncomfortable underpinnings; thus the eaglets are forced to leave the nest and develop flight skills.

The whole physical universe is full of examples that speak of the value of sometimes painful discipline. No horse is useful until it is harnessed. No steam or gas ever drives an engine until it is confined. Niagara Falls cannot produce light and power until its power is harnessed.

Likewise, no human life can become great until it is focused, dedicated, and disciplined. Such maturity can result from trials in life, properly accepted. Just as the struggles of moths and eaglets provide for their natural development, so also our hardships are designed by God for our spiritual development. "The testing of your faith through trials develops perseverance... so that you may be mature and complete," James assures us (Jas 1:3-4).

You have probably noticed, however, that not everyone matures through the adversities and hurts of life. Pain can cause some people to turn against God in bitterness. For these, suffering is not a stepping-stone but a stumbling block; it's a grindstone grinding them down rather than polishing them up. Those who accept God's pruning, produce; those who reject it grow sour grapes. There's nothing like real tribulation to separate the faith-hardy from the faith-weak. (Appropriately enough, the word tribulation comes from the Latin word *tribulum*, which means a rod used to beat the grain to separate the kernel from the chaff.) Tribulations sift the mature from the immature.

And so we must make a careful distinction here. It is not suffering in itself that brings about growth. The essential element is to be intimately linked with Christ in the closest union of love as hardships come upon us. Pruning causes fruitfulness *only* in those branches which are nourished by grace-sap flowing from the Vine. As Jesus said, "No branch can bear fruit by itself; it must remain in the vine. Neither can you bear fruit *unless you remain in me*" (Jn 15:4).

How do we know whether or not we are remaining in Christ? "If anyone does not have the Spirit of Christ, he does not belong to [remain in] Christ," Paul answers (Rom 8:9). He intimates that those who are not in Christ include those who are "hostile to God" (8:7). Hence, anyone resisting God's will and plan because it involves suffering is a branch that does not remain in Christ, the Vine, and thus is not fruitful. Such a one has no future. "My Father... cuts off every branch in me that bears no fruit," says Jesus. And further, "If anyone does not remain in me, he is like a branch that is thrown away and withers; such branches are picked up, thrown into the fire and burned" (Jn 15:2, 6).

SUFFERING—WAY TO GROW

But, we ask, precisely *how* do the trials and adversities of life bring about the growth that makes us spiritually mature and complete? To answer this question we have only to look at the fruit from the fruitful branch, that is, the branch vibrant with Jesus' Spirit. "The fruit of the Spirit is love, joy, peace, patience, kindness, goodness, faithfulness, gentleness and self-control" (Gal 5:22-23). Only in the womb of adversity can these fruits of the Spirit be developed.

It is easy to *say* we have love for others, for example. But what happens when that love is tested? What happens when someone offends us by theft, injury, rape, or embezzlement? In the face of such adversity does love for the offender thrive undiminished in our soul? If so, the trial produces enormous growth. Try the test of joy. What happens when we meet with unexpected tragedy or a big disappointment? If our soul-based joy perdures, then this very climate of adversity is yielding marvelous fruit. What about inner peace? Is it undisturbed by irksome and worrisome trials? Then such trials are working as a strengthening agent.

If we were never tempted to impatience, could we ever develop the virtue of patience? Does our kindness flourish in the face of harshness directed against us? Does our goodness grow in the face of evil that surrounds us as we follow Paul's injunction, "Do not be overcome by evil, but overcome evil with good" (Rom 12:21)? Do we remain faithful when surrounded by faithless people at work or elsewhere? Are we self-controlled in dealing with the allurements of gluttony, addictions, or lust? If so, then all these hardships redound to our spiritual growth.

Even when we are not fully cooperative with God's plan to

use adversity in our lives—that is, if we fall low on the six-level scale of faith—still his plan is not altogether frustrated. We may fail God, but he does not fail us. Even the very painful awareness of our faith-weakness can be used by God to help us grow in humility. God is faithful, and he will build on even a miniscule bit of good will: "He who began a good work in you will carry it on to completion" (Phil 1:6).

Our spiritual growth is in the hands of a loving God who knows us intimately and has designed a tailor-made plan for our good. Another example from nature comes to mind here. A hen has four different sounds to call her brood: one at dusk to warn of approaching nightfall; one to call them to feed; one to alert them to impending danger; and one simply to call them to herself. All of these calls are designed for the chicks' ultimate benefit. So too, all of the multiform afflictions sent or allowed by God are for our ultimate benefit ultimately; each is engineered to fit a given situation, time, personality, or spiritual need. Our custom-designed sufferings reflect God's consummate respect for our unique individuality.

A doctor does not prescribe the same medicine for every patient; each patient has different health needs. Likewise, God chooses uniquely designed afflictions for each of us. My cross is not the same as your cross; yours fits your needs most perfectly, mine fits my needs. But no one is cross-free. "We *all* must go through many hardships to enter the kingdom of God" (Acts 14:22).

Again, every single hardship—from the annoyance of a traffic jam to a death in the family—is designed to help us grow in some way. If it were not beneficial medicine, God would not prescribe it, "for he does not willingly bring affliction or grief to the children of men" (Lam 3:33). God allows only those sufferings he deems necessary. Like a parent subjecting a child to painful surgery, he does not hesitate to subject us to hurts designed for our spiritual health or growth.

So let us not try to be affliction-resistant souls! (Such people remind me of the patient who followed only that part of the directions on his medicine bottle that said, "Keep bottle tightly closed.") On the contrary, let us determine to benefit as fully as possible from God's medicine, distasteful though we may find it. These directions may be helpful:

1. *Submit to any part of the suffering that is unavoidable*—not reluctantly, as a defeated general might submit to his conqueror, but *voluntarily*, as a patient eager for health submits to the prospect of surgery. Submit *joyfully*, like a woman awaiting childbirth even though she dreads the birth pains. If God's plan in your pain is evident, respond with humble *obedience*; if not evident, respond with humble *faith*.

2. *Bring the word of God to bear on the situation.* The Scriptures teach us how to respond to adversities; conversely, adversities can help us to respond to the insights of Scripture. In this way, "head knowledge" about the art of suffering can become "heart knowledge." God's personal loving concern for you may become meaningful as you ponder passages such as Isaiah 43:1-5: "I have summoned you by name; you are mine. When you pass through the waters I will be with you.... When you walk through the fire you will not be burned.... You are precious and honored.... I love you.... Do not be afraid, for I am with you."

3. *Trust God blindly through all hardships.* Be like Job, who said, "Though he slay me, yet will I trust him" (Jb13:15). In trust too, there are degrees. Dwight L. Moody, the celebrated preacher, once said, "You can travel to heaven by either first or second class. Second class is for those who say, 'When I am afraid I will trust.' First class is for those who say, 'I will trust and *not* be afraid'" (see Isaiah 12:2).

4. *Remember the lessons learned from past suffering.* Don't simply endure trials; call them to mind—not only as past sorrows but as soul disciplines. Moses told the Israelites, "*Remember* how the Lord led you in the desert these forty years to *humble* you and *test* you... causing you to hunger... to teach you that man does not live on bread alone, but on every word

that comes from the mouth of the Lord.... As a man disciplines his son, so the Lord disciplines you" (Dt 8:2-5). This
kind of memory-freshening is vital when our cross gets heavy.

HEAVEN'S VIEW OF A CROSS

Growth in Christlike holiness is the hallmark of each cross
along the "cross-road" to Calvary. A sinless Virgin's heart was
pierced with a sword of sorrow, watching the heart of her sinless
Son pierced with a lance. Shall we who are not sinless resent
being pierced with God's well-disguised redemptive love?

The art of suffering can be mastered by looking at it with a
God's-eye view. No one has put that view into words better
than St. Francis de Sales in his classic prayer card gem, "Your
Cross":

> The everlasting God has in his wisdom foreseen from eternity
> the cross he now presents to you as a gift from his inmost
> heart. This cross he now sends you he has gazed at with his
> all-knowing eyes, understood with his divine mind, tested
> with his wise justice, warmed with his loving arms, and
> weighed with his own hands, to see that it be not one inch
> too large and not one ounce too heavy for *you*. He has
> blessed it with his holy name, anointed it with his grace, per-
> fumed it with his consolation, taken one last glance at you
> and your courage, and then sent it to you from heaven—a
> special greeting from God to you, an alms of the all-merciful
> love of God. That is **YOUR CROSS!**[1]

A modern mystic with a similar God-view penned a poem
while being forged in the crucible of suffering. He was a
Trappist monk, and he handed me a copy of his poem while I
was visiting his community to conduct a retreat on the theme of
suffering. I quote his poem here as a fitting capstone to these
reflections on suffering.

The Kiss of Christ

Lo, there He hangs —
Ashened figure pinioned against the wood.
God grant that I might love Him
Even as I should.

I draw a little closer
To feel His love divine,
And hear Him gently whisper,
"Ah, precious child of mine —

If now I should embrace you,
My hands would stain you red,
And if I leaned to whisper,
My thorns would pierce your head."

'Twas there I learned in sorrow
That love demands a price;
'Twas then I learned that suffering
Is but the kiss of Christ.

THIRTEEN

Three Ways to Carry a Cross

The tin can was invented in 1810. The can opener was invented fifty-five years later.

Problems are often with us for a long time before solutions are found. The all-pervasive problem of human suffering had been around long before Job, who struggled to find a solution and ultimately discovered it in trusting in divine providence. But the fullest grasp of that solution was not available until much later through the example of Jesus.

Jesus was well acquainted with the problem of suffering and knew before it happened that he would drink of this cup (the cup or chalice is a traditional scriptural symbol of deep suffering: see Psalm 75:18; Ezekiel 23:31-34). Jesus predicted his own suffering, along with a challenge: "Can you drink the cup I am going to drink?" (Mt 20:22). Later in his agony he prayed three times, "If it be possible may this cup be taken from me. Yet, not as I will, but as you will" (Mt 26:39-44). Having foreseen the inevitable, still Jesus asked to be exempted from it. (Job had made a similar request; see his parallel prayer in Job 6:8-9).

Jesus' prayer strikes us as enigmatic—and we are even more mystified by the fact that Scripture says his prayer was heard: "He offered up prayers and petitions to the one who could save him from death, and *he was heard* because of his reverent submission" (Heb 5:7).

But Jesus died a torturous death! In what sense can we say his prayer was heard? This question has been puzzled over and analyzed for centuries by Scripture scholars, who have come up with three possible explanations or "solutions," each of which might also provide spiritual insights for dealing with our own sufferings. These insights may be called three ways to carry a cross. Separately or together, they may help us bear our personal crosses.

FIRST SOLUTION: SUBMISSION TO GOD'S WILL

Jesus' human nature rebelled against pain, for he was like us in every way, he has been through suffering, and knows what it is like when we suffer (see Hebrews 2:17-18). And again, "We do not have a high priest who is unable to sympathize with us, but one who has been tempted in every way, just as we are—yet without sin" (Heb 4:15). Challenged to obey God's will in supreme sacrifice, Jesus "learned obedience [to God's will] from what he suffered" (Heb 5:8). The same letter follows up with some pastoral advice; "Let us fix our eyes on Jesus, who, for the joy set before him endured the cross.... Consider him... so that you will not grow weary and lose heart" (Heb 12:2-3).

As we identify with Jesus, the paradigm of submission to God's will in suffering, we can hear his follow-up prayer echoing through our soul: "Not as I will, but as you will." This attitude had characterized his whole earthly life, for his very conception had been God's response to submission on the part of Mary: "Be it done to me according to your word [God's will]." And now Jesus was practicing what he had taught his followers to pray: "Thy will be done on earth..."

But was Jesus' prayer for release from suffering really answered? Yes, says this first solution, because his prayer was ultimately a prayer for the accomplishment of the divine will, to which his human will was submitted. In the light of this first solution the key phrase is: "He was heard *because of his reverent submission*" to God's will (Heb 5:7). To paraphrase it, Jesus' prayer was: "I want relief, but only if it is your will. My human will is ultimately and absolutely submitted to your divine will."

The "if it be possible" part of his prayer was uttered also in this same context. Knowing that "all things are possible to God" (Mt 19:26; Lk 1:37), Jesus prayed, in effect, "If it be possible *without contravening your divine plan.*" Jesus prayed conditionally in suffering, which is not usually our tendency. For most of us the phrase "Thy will be done on earth" is all too often eclipsed by the urgency of our petition, "Give us this day..." Especially in suffering, God's will is mostly a background experience, while our needs have a foreground focus. With Jesus, this was reversed.

This gives us another perspective on the question we are examining. Perhaps we are beginning to understand how, or in what sense, Jesus' prayer was heard. Now we can reformulate the question—*why* was it heard? John 5:14 provides the answer: "If we ask anything *according to his will*, he hears us."

What then is "according to God's will"? Not sickness, for there is no scriptural indication that sickness ("intrinsic" suffering) is according to God's will—with the rare exception of "redemptive" human suffering in illness, to which very few are called. In fact, we should almost always presume that God wants healing from sickness.

"Extrinsic" suffering, however, *is* according to God's permissive will. Caused by such things as persecution, social injustice, an unloving spouse, inclement weather, and accidents, this kind of suffering is what Jesus had in mind when he said that each of his followers must "take up his cross and follow me" (Mt 16:24).

Jesus' suffering was of the extrinsic type. But how could it be according to God's will that Jesus should suffer? Why would any loving father want his beloved son to suffer? Similarly, does God really want us to suffer? Does he gloat over our sufferings as if they provide some form of divine fulfillment? Does our suffering really fulfill God's will, and thus make him happy? By no means. For all such questions, the bottom line is: God sometimes wills our suffering *permissively,* but never *positively.* Moreover, he wills it as a means, not as an end in itself. By analogy, you may *permissively* will to take a fatiguing flight to Hawaii for a vacation that you *positively* will or desire.

God permissively willed Jesus' suffering for many reasons. He desired to show vividly the extent of redemptive love (see John 15:13—"Greater love has no one than this...") and to elicit our repentance through it. He willed it as an example for us of patience, fortitude, forgiveness. Likewise, God permissively wills *our* suffering for many reasons (one theologian listed nineteen reasons referred to in Scripture).

Like us, Paul sought a solution to the perplexing problem of suffering: "We are hard-pressed on every side, but not crushed; *perplexed,* but not in despair" (2 Cor 4:9). But Paul did detect God's good purposes at work—among them, inward renewal through suffering and, above all, an overwhelmingly disproportionate reward (see 2 Corinthians 4:16-17; Romans 8:18). Peter emphasizes this advantage also (see 1 Peter 1:6) and adds other reasons for suffering. And so, when we too are perplexed we might consider that our cross may redound to good in some unexpected way (see Romans 8:28; Isaiah 38:17; Jeremiah 29:11; Philippians 1:19). As we meditate on all this, we will see the problem of suffering in proper perspective; then, embracing God's will in suffering will be less difficult. With Jesus as our great exemplar (see 1 Peter 4:1-2) our bitter trials will become bittersweet, and they will grow sweeter and sweeter as we hunger more and more for God's will in our suffering.

SECOND SOLUTION: NOT ABORTING GOD'S WILL

A second interpretation of "May this cup be taken from me" is that Jesus was simply praying not to die before his appointed time, since that would abort God's plan and fulfill Satan's will. Satan feared Christ's prophesied crucifixion as the culminating act of redemption. Thus when Jesus exclaimed, "My soul is overwhelmed with sorrow to the point of death" (Mt 26:38; Mk 14:34), the man of sorrows may have felt that this incomprehensible burden of the sins of all humanity was about to kill him before he could even be crucified. "He poured out his life unto [up to the point of] death... for he bore the sin of many" (Is 53:12). Jesus showed that he wanted to fulfill the prophecies and carry out God's will, for he reminded his apostles that he could have called for twelve legions of angels to prevent his arrest, "but how then would the Scriptures be fulfilled that say it must happen in this way?" (Mt 26:54). "Shall I not drink the cup the Father has given me?" (18:11).

So perhaps Jesus was really praying that his death would not be premature when he asked that the cup be spared him. The Father responded by sending an angel to strengthen him until the crucifixion (Lk 22:43). Thus, a premature, sorrow-caused death was averted, Jesus' prayer was answered, and Satan was thwarted. "'Now the prince of this world will be driven out. But I, when I be lifted up [on the cross] will draw all men to myself.' He said this to show what kind of death he was going to die" (Jn 12:31-33). Clearly, Jesus connected Satan's expulsion with his own death by crucifixion. He knew that he was not born to live but born to die; this is why he protested that he was not trying to avoid death itself: "What shall I say? 'Father, save me from this hour'? No, it was for this very reason I came to this hour" (Jn 12:27).

What about us? In our own personal sufferings, are we aborting God's will in some way? We are if we lack perseverance. "Blessed is the man who perseveres under trial, because when he has stood the test, he will receive the crown of life" (Jas 1:12). "You need to persevere, so that when you have done the will of God, you will receive what he has promised" (Heb 10:36).

We also abort God's will by our resistance or even by our lack of joy in suffering. "Consider it pure joy, my brothers, whenever you face trials of many kinds" (Jas 1:2). It may be hard to rejoice in our sufferings, but a reminder from Jesus helps: "Blessed are you when people insult you and persecute you... rejoice and be glad, because great is your reward in heaven" (Mt 5:11-12). But the most spiritual motive is stated by Peter: "Rejoice that you participate in the suffering of Christ" (1 Pt 4:13).

Failures to persevere and rejoice are only two of the ways by which we can abort God's will in suffering. But with Christ as our guide, we can leave such failures behind and grow into a mature approach to suffering that can transform every cross into a paradoxical blend of sorrow and joy.

THIRD SOLUTION: COMPLETING GOD'S WILL

There is a third interpretation as to how Christ's Gethsemane prayer was answered. This solution maintains that Jesus prayed to be saved from death (if such was the Father's will, of course) and that the Father heard Jesus' prayer and answered it—not by saving Jesus from death, but *out from* death; that is, by raising him from death on Easter Sunday. This interpretation holds that Jesus asked for the *prevention* of his death but that the Father sent him instead a *"cure"* of his death: "Death has been swallowed up in victory" (1 Cor 15:54; Is 25:8). It is as if someone who is slowly going blind asks for a cure but still goes blind, only to be miraculously healed of blindness later—thus giving greater glory to God by a more dramatic miracle.

This interesting interpretation, like the first two, also suggests an approach for how we might carry our cross. We may pray for relief from suffering and find that God seems not to answer our prayer. Perhaps we are praying for a healing of terminal cancer for ourselves or for a loved one and find that death comes ineluctably. To a worldling, that looks like an unanswered prayer. But death itself is the most beautiful of all healings, when we find life on the other side indescribably better than on this side. "O death, your sentence is welcome to the man who is in need and whose strength fails" (Sir 41:3). While death is a beautiful healing that is meant to catapult us into the arms of God, our subsequent resurrection of the body (see 1 Thessalonians 4:16; 1 Corinthians 15:51-52) is a further healing. Then our glorified body is united with our soul (see John 5:29), as we see in Jesus, the first of those to be "cured" of death, or resurrected (see 1 Corinthians 15:20). Every cross of ours is meant to point to an open tomb, "for the same God who brought Jesus back from death will also bring us back to life again with Jesus" (2 Cor 4:14).

In all our sufferings we must never lose sight of what might lie ahead, in God's plan. We should seek the *completing* of God's will more than an immediate response to our needs. "Those who suffer according to God's will should commit themselves to their faithful Creator and *continue* doing good" (1 Pt 4:19). God does not seem to be answering your prayers for a certain job? He may have a better job lined up for you weeks or months from now—one in which you will meet your future spouse, perhaps, or lead a fellow worker to the Lord, or avoid a serious injury you might have sustained on the job you are praying for now. "'My ways are not your ways,' declares the Lord" (Is 55:8). And so your apparently unanswered prayer for God to "take away the cup" may ultimately be answered in another way, just as Jesus' resurrection was possibly the answer to his prayer for deliverance from imminent death.

And so these three "solutions" to the question of how Jesus' Gethsemane prayer was answered can provide a perspective on how we can carry our cross in a Christlike way. Whichever way or combination of ways you may choose, remember that Jesus suffers not just *for* us (see Matthew 8:17) but also *with* us (see 1 Peter 4:13). In a way, this makes Jesus our Simon of Cyrene who helps us to carry our cross. In this light, our suffering takes on the nature of a privilege.

FOURTEEN

Coping with Life's Darkest Moments

Put on your thinking cap for a moment. Quickly, choose any number between one and ten. Double it. Add six. Divide by two. Subtract your original number. The remainder is three. If you want, try it with every number between one and ten. The remainder will always be three.

In this puzzling computation, as in life, the important thing is not what you start with but the process. The answer to any "problem" of life is usually not difficult; the trick is to follow the "process" of living that will lead to the answer.

Much of this process of living is a matter of "processing" problems—knowing how to cope with trials, hardships, and difficulties. In heaven there are no trials or stress, so there we won't have to cope; we can "rest in peace." But here on earth we meet with adversities, tribulations, and hardships, which we tend to think of as periods of darkness. The darkest parts of these trials we regard as "midnight events"—they are often preceded by some threatening darkness and followed by periods of depressing darkness. Thus, the foreboding fear of losing a job becomes the midnight of being fired, followed by the dark depression of extended unemployment. The fear of cancer precedes the midnight of the shocking lab report, followed by the darkness of suffering or painful treatment. For those who are terminally ill, each day has its own midnight as they anticipate the touch of the cold hand of death; the survivors experience midnights of bereavement, possibly preceded by the dark task of nursing a sick loved one, and followed by dark loneliness in their loss. Most trials climax with a seemingly intense darkness.

God in his mercy keeps most of the future veiled from our eyes; yet we can't keep from wondering what inevitable midnights that future holds for us and how we will cope with those darkest moments. We know they will come, for Jesus reminds us that *"each day* has troubles of its own" (Mt 6:34). So with this predetermined, like the final number on our math trick, we can realistically expect quite a number of midnights within any given time frame. But while the inevitable answer, suffering, is known and recognized as unavoidable, what is not always considered is the process—that is, the coping process. The trick is to go through midnights seeing light with your heart while your eyes see only darkness. As one quipster put it, "Real faith is the ability to let your light shine after your fuse is blown." So how exactly can we best cope with life's inevitable midnights?

Perhaps as a symbolic preview of life's hardships, each new year begins precisely at midnight—with nighttime preceding and following it. But there is also a dawn on New Year's Day, counterpointing the darkness with joyous events like the world-famous Tournament of Roses parade and football games. All of life is thus checkered—not all darkness nor all light; not all bitter nor all sweet, but bittersweet. Any adversity can be hyphenated with joy, and darkness with light. And to see that light at the end of the tunnel is simply to practice the Christian virtue of hope—optimism based on God's loving providence that "works in all things for the good of those who love him" (Rom 8:28). Such an attitude leaves no room for the facetious advice of the pessimist who advocated eating dessert first, since life is so uncertain!

Scripture is replete with significant events that occurred literally at midnight—most of them illuminated with a heavenly intervention—to show that no dark event need be without divine light. We know that Jesus was born at night (see Luke 2:8)—at the very hour of midnight, according to a pious tradition. He who called himself the Light of the world burst incandescently into that sin-darkened world to which heaven-sent angels announced a message of peace. He suggested that when he returns in bright glory, it *may* be at midnight (see Mark 13:35). He expressed this in a parable featuring a bridegroom's surprise return at midnight (see Matthew 25:6).

It was at the promised midnight hour that God sent the tenth plague on Egypt, slaying the firstborn of every Egyptian family and of their cattle (see Exodus 12:29). This was the momentous event that opened the way for the Exodus, the Israelites' escape from generations of slavery—an historic event that prototyped the climactic event of our redemption.

It was at midnight that God awoke Samson to surprise the unprepared Philistines (see Judges 16:3). It was at midnight that Ruth was discovered and protected by Boaz, who was awakened at that hour (see Ruth 3:8). It was at midnight that the litigant woman's child was kidnapped but later restored to her by Solomon's judicial wisdom (see 1 Kings 3:20). Elihu reminded Job that death can come to anyone at midnight (see Job 34:20); yet death is not an end but a beginning of eternal life. The psalmist chose midnight for his deepest prayer: "At midnight I rise to give thanks to you, O Lord" (Ps 119:62). It was the midnight importuning of the breadless neighbor in Jesus' parable that produced a favorable response (see Luke 11:5). The midnight prison prayer of Paul and Silas produced an earthquake that burst open the prison doors and converted the jailer (see Acts 16:25). Later, in Troas, it was the midnight hour when Paul worked his greatest miracle in raising Eutychus from the dead (see Acts 20:7).

In all these biblical events, the dark midnight hour was counterposed against a glimmering if not dazzling brightness of

God's intervention. In our midnight trials we too can have a profound, faith-spawned insight about God's supportive presence amidst our darkest hardships. As some sage has said: "Joy is not the absence of suffering but the presence of God."

Just as the proverbial dark cloud has a silver lining, so every dark midnight has a background glow—but only for those who see the hand of God bringing good from all of life's hurtful events. "'I know the plans I have for you,' declares the Lord, 'plans to prosper you and not to harm you, plans to give you hope and a future'" (Jer 29:11). Without the ability to recognize God's involvement in our life and his concern for us in our trials, there is no divine brilliance to offset the tribulatory gloom. God's hurt is seeing that his loving presence is unrecognized by us.

In the Jerusalem of Jesus' day, this loving presence went unrecognized by most of the city's inhabitants. Jesus wept over the city, foreseeing its destruction forty years later "because *you did not recognize the time of God's coming to you.*" (In fact, Jerusalem has been attacked twenty-four times and destroyed nineteen times and has seldom known the peace the psalmist urges us to pray for.) Through his tears Jesus lamented: "If you had only known what would bring you peace—but now it is hidden from your eyes" (Lk 19:41-44).

But the Bible also presents some darksome situations that were transformed through openness to God's help. In the days of the high priest Azariah, for example, "it was not safe to travel about, for all the inhabitants of the lands were in great turmoil. One nation was being crushed by another, because God was troubling them with every kind of distress" (2 Chr 15:5-6). Then the Spirit inspired Azariah to convince King Asa to turn himself and his kingdom over to the Lord's care. Asa did so, and with his national religious revival God sent peace to the land for years.

We in today's world are in turmoil far worse than in biblical times. In our drug-dazed, violence-saturated, crime-ridden society, it can also be hard to see God's loving presence. A midnight darkness blankets mankind like a morbid pall. As a token attempt at dealing with this, January first has been designated as World Peace Day. But that fact is hardly recognized or adverted to by most people. Nor is there any sign of a God-fearing, leader-inspired religious revival to parallel the one that was led by King Asa. Ironically, the very organization set up to secure world peace, the United Nations, has yet to recognize the Prince of Peace.

But whether we consider the darkness of worldwide turmoil or just the turmoil within our own personal or family life, we must harbor hope of God's shedding his blessed light of love on us in our midnights of trial and adversity. Otherwise, an incurable malady may develop: "Hope deferred makes the heart sick" (Prv 13:12). Without the light of hope we miss the revelation of God's love, and "where there is no revelation, the people cast off restraint" (Prv 29:18). Isn't this what we see happening across the face of our society today? People are missing God's love-whispers and casting off all restraint—with catastrophic results.

SKYLIGHT OF HOPE

Stars can be seen only at night, and the darker the night the greater the number of visible stars. In all our darkest trials, we must learn to highlight each midnight with starlight through the skylight of hope. And so, in our hours of darkness the best outlook is an uplook—an uplook through the skylight of hope, from which we can see the Christ-star which will guide us, as it did the Magi, to the Prince of Peace. For truly Christ-focused Christians, the darker the midnight events in their personal life—or in the world at large—the brighter glows the star of hope. With David they exclaim, "I trust in you, O Lord.... My times are in your hands.... Save me in your unfailing love" (Ps 31:14-16).

At the beginning of each day, week, or month it might be

appropriate to take a survey of just how strongly we believe in God and his love for us, especially in our "midnight" situations, when he can seem so absent. Again, Paul's challenge is helpful: "Examine yourselves to see whether you are in the faith; test yourselves. Do you not *realize* that Christ Jesus is in you— unless, of course, you fail the test?" (2 Cor 13:5). Try this test by asking a somewhat harsh question: In the dark periods of life, do I respond more like an atheist or like a Christian? Perhaps your answer will crystallize as you ponder the following little item written by an anonymous professed atheist of the eighteenth century, "If I Believed":

> *If* I firmly believed, as millions say they do, that the knowledge and practice of religion in this life influence destiny in another life, then religion would mean to me everything. I would cast away earthly enjoyments as dross, earthly cares as folly, and earthly thoughts and feelings as vanity. God would be my first waking thought and my last image before falling asleep. I would labor in his cause alone. I would hardly stop thinking of my future eternity. I would regard the saving of one soul worth a life of suffering; earthly consequences would never prevent me from acting or speaking out to accomplish this. The griefs of life would occupy hardly a moment of my thoughts. I would go forth to the world and preach this message in season and out of season, and my scripture text would be: "What does it profit a man if he gain the whole world and lose his own soul?" All of this would overwhelmingly preoccupy me—that is, *if* I believed!

As this atheist points out, real faith would help a person to see earthly life from the perspective of eternity; even grief "would occupy hardly a moment of my thoughts," he says. Most of us do not usually act as though we had this kind of faith! Yet it is what mature Christians are called to. Paul, for example, demonstrated this "spirit of faith" in dealing with the agonizing midnights of his own life.

We do not lose heart. Though outwardly we are wasting away, yet inwardly we are being renewed day by day. For our light and momentary troubles are achieving for us an eternal glory that far outweighs them all. So we fix our eyes not on what is seen, but on what is unseen. For what is seen is temporary, but what is unseen is eternal.

2 Corinthians 4:16-18

Peter is another example of faith in the midst of adversity. Like Paul's, his advice often has an eschatological ring: "Rejoice that you participate in the sufferings of Christ, so that you may be overjoyed when his glory is revealed.... Those who suffer according to God's will should commit themselves to their faithful Creator and continue to do good" (1 Pt 4:19). As we learn to cope with life's midnight experiences, we too will become more able to focus on God and to see the present and future benefits of our suffering.

A THREEFOLD CONSOLATION IN DESOLATION

Suffering can be greatly meritorious and yet it can easily camouflage the presence of God in the soul. As we become more and more Spirit-filled, though, it becomes easier to find meaning in the ever-present sufferings of life. We see that each Person of the Trinity, in his own way, shines a divine light on one or other of the many facets of the diamond of suffering to bring out its iridescence and beauty.

When we're really hurting, like a youngster with a skin-scrape after a fall, we might be inspired to let our heavenly Father sweep us into his loving arms and smother us with loving compassion and tender paternal care, all the while reminding us that ultimately everything will be all right. He gently encourages us to trust in him with perfect abandonment to his will in every trial and tribulation that befalls us, even when we can't see the reason for it.

The Father may help us to understand that by allowing us to land flat on our back in sickness and pain he forces us to take time to look up. As C.S. Lewis put it, "God whispers to us in our pleasures; he speaks to us in our work; but he shouts to us in our pain"[1]—which is often the very time we refuse to listen. In the midst of a hardship it's not easy to believe the words of Jeremiah: "Though the Lord brings grief, he will show compassion, so great is his unfailing love. For he does not willingly bring affliction or grief to the children of men" (Lam 3:31). Still, this is the truth!

Jesus may relate to us differently than the Father does. In our suffering he might remind us of his promise: "In this world you will have trouble. But take heart! I have overcome the world" (Jn 16:33). He might dissolve our self-pity as we view a crucifix while trying—unsuccessfully—to imagine him uttering our own self-pitying words, "What did *I* do to deserve this?" Or he may show us that we are afraid to offer our bodies "as living sacrifices, holy and pleasing to God" (Rom 12:1).

Jesus may show us how suffering can work to disengage us from sinful habits. He may encourage you to *"rejoice* that you participate in the sufferings of Christ, so that you may be overjoyed when his glory is revealed" (1 Pt 4:13). Or he may reveal a transcendent meaning in suffering, as he did to his apostles: "This sickness... is for God's glory, so that God's Son may be glorified through it" (Jn 11:4). His beatitudinal words may echo through our minds in the face of opposition: "Blessed are you when people insult you, persecute you and falsely say all kinds of evil against you... rejoice and be glad, because great is your reward in heaven" (Mt 5:11-12).

The Holy Spirit, whom Jesus called the Comforter, ministers comfort to us in our trials: "The Lord comforts his people and will have compassion on his afflicted ones" (Is 49:13). A forceful Hebrew construction highlights his personal compassion: *"I, even I,* am he who comforts you" (Is 51:12). There is a note of tenderness here too: "As a mother comforts her child, so will I comfort you" (Is 66:13). Through the Holy Spirit we have a standing offer of his great gift of fortitude in our sufferings (see Isaiah 11:2). He intercedes for our relief by praying through us himself with the gift of tongues: "The Spirit helps us in our weakness [afflictions].... [he] himself intercedes for us with groans that words cannot express" (Rom 8:26).

From this it should be clear that the one triune God functions in our souls with the varied patterns of each Person in the Trinity. This triune God-presence offers us a spectrum of divine dynamics to make us truly God-like: God's indwelling presence, Spirit-baptism, inspirations of grace, support in suffering, and countless other forms of divine involvement. All these expressions of God's love don't come to us merely occasionally. We are being blessed minute by minute with his gifts, with every breath we take.

Since God uses suffering for our sanctification and his glory if we endure it in accordance with his will and designs, any given moment—painful or joyful—can be consecrated to him and thus redound enormously to our advantage. This is why Peter can urge, "Cast *all* your anxiety on him, for he cares for you" (1 Pt 5:7; Ps 55:22). This involves a kind of trustful commitment: *"Commit* your way to the Lord; trust in him" (Ps 37:5). Thus, the darkest midnight experiences of your coming weeks, months, or years are special opportunities to offer the Lord this commitment of surrender to his providence.

TWO QUESTIONS ASKED BY THE FAINT-HEARTED

In the midst of sufferings, all but the most God-trusting souls tend to ask two questions: 1) Why this suffering, or at least why now, Lord?; and 2) How long will this darkness last, Lord?

Typical of the first plaint are questions such as: Why are my prayers unavailing? Why do I have the spiritual "blahs"? Why am I assailed with such overwhelming temptations? Why can't the doctors do something for me or my sick loved ones? Why can't I find happiness in marriage? Why can't I find a job? Why is my life so unfulfilled? Why am I so depressed?

Typical of the second category of questions are such grievance queries as: When will this pain end? How long will I feel lonely? Will my son ever conquer his drug addiction? How long must I endure the misery of living with an unrecovered alcoholic spouse? Will I ever be able to get out of debt?

Look again at the remarks of the atheist who theorized about what his behavior would be if he were to come to have faith. "The griefs of life would occupy hardly a moment of my thoughts." Doesn't the contrast with our plaintive questions convict us of our faith-weakness in the face of suffering? Certainly these midnight events of life are real. Yet their positive potential is also real. If our suffering is not being fully utilized, if we are indulging in querulous questions, this aborts to some extent the grace proffered to us in our dark moments. How much grace we cheat ourselves of by our reluctance to embrace God's will!

God reprimanded Job because his complaints in his suffering were "words without knowledge," as Job himself admitted (see Job 38:2; 42:3) The Lord asked him if he intended to let his unthinking questions lead him to deny God's loving providence. This is the temptation we face too. It is precisely in the midst of such darkness that our faith is most pointedly challenged. Just as storms deepen the root system of a windblown oak, so the storms of adversity are designed to root us deeper in our faith. Only an intrepid and stalwart Christ-focused faith that perdures through our dark storms will help us to accept Paul's assertion that for those who love God and fit into his plans, all such things "work together unto good" (Rom 8:28).

To let the Lord focus the spotlight of his loving providence on the dark moments of your life, try this simple prayer of surrender:

Lord, you've got the whole world in your hands. And now, Lord, you've got my problems in your hands—my seemingly insoluble problems that I have been worrying over incessantly. They look like big problems to me, Lord, but nothing's too big for you. If you can keep the earth spinning and keep the galaxies in place, if you can supervise all creation, I guess you can manage my problems. My task is to refrain from worrying now; I've just got to trust you, believe you, love you. Help me to let go—to surrender to your loving providence in my life. Don't let me interfere with your solution to what were once my problems. They're yours now, Lord—these unique, special problems. Take them, please, and solve them in your own way and in your own time. Thank you, Lord. Amen.

FIFTEEN

Speak Up, Lord—I Can't Hear You!

A man drives away from a roadside gas station, absent-mindedly leaving his wife there after a bathroom stop. A police car retrieves his irate wife and eventually catches up with the husband. Exclaims the grateful husband to the policeman, "Thank God! I thought I was going deaf!"

To a person who is really deaf, a hearing impairment is seldom a joking matter. But of all forms of deafness, the most serious is spiritual deafness—the inability to hear the voice of God in the many ways he communicates with us, especially through his incarnate Word, Jesus. The author of Hebrews opens his letter by giving an update on this very latest in Creator-creature communication—a more dramatic communication breakthrough than the invention of printing: "In the past God spoke to our forefathers through the prophets at many times and in various ways, but in these last days he has spoken to us by his Son, whom he has appointed heir of all things, and through whom he made the universe" (Heb 1:1-2).

SPIRITUAL DEAFNESS AMONG GOD'S PEOPLE

Euripides felt that silence was a wise man's answer, and Plutarch said it was an answer to fools. Both these views of silence could be applied to God's exercise of punitive noncommunication during Israel's long period of judges. "In those days the word of the Lord was rare" (1 Sm 3:1). Throughout that time he spoke through only two prophets and one prophetess (Deborah). "For a long time Israel was without a priest to teach and without the law. But in *their distress* they turned to the Lord and he was found by them" (2 Chr 15:3-4). Shakespeare might have been describing God's strategy when he wrote the intuitive words: "Silence often persuades when speaking fails."

Apparently spiritual hearing was also poor during the age of Israel's prophets. They were persecuted for their utterances, as Jesus reminds us (see Matthew 5:12; Luke 6:23). And Jesus himself seems to have fared little better than those beleaguered prophets in making himself heard against the hissing and howling discordance of his own persecutors (see John 15:20).

Most of mankind doesn't want to listen to God, it seems—and yet when God grows silent, "the natives grow restless." There's an instinctive need we all have to *hear* from God occasionally, even if we don't really *listen* to him. Hearing is not necessarily listening, and listening is not necessarily heeding. But when God is silent for too long we feel a certain distress and also tend to become morally lax.

In the coming end times, God's non-revelation will seem to be a severe silence, certainly more punitive than in the days of Israel's judges. The prophet Amos gave a gripping description of such times:

"The days are coming," declares the Sovereign Lord, "when I will send a famine through the land—not a famine of food or a thirst for water, but a famine of hearing the words of the Lord. Men will stagger, searching for the word of the Lord, but they will not find it."   **Amos 8:11-12**

HOW TO LISTEN TO GOD'S VOICE

To immunize ourselves against that dreaded time as much as possible, we might well review one of the Bible's best lessons on the art of listening to God—the story of the boy Samuel, whose ability to hear the voice of God later made him a strong prophetic voice among his people. He started with a triple handicap: first, he lived at a time when "the word of the Lord was rare" (1 Sm 3:1); second, "Samuel did not yet know the Lord" (1 Sm 3:7); and third, three times he mistook the very voice of God for the human voice of his mentor, Eli. With those three strikes, he should have struck out. But patiently God tried still another pitch, and this time Samuel made a hit. Why? Because little Samuel was finally coached by Eli to respond with the right words to God's word: "Speak, Lord, for your servant is listening" (1 Sam 3:9).With lowly simplicity he identified himself as the Lord's *servant* (the very word bespeaks humble obedience, and parallels Mary's "handmaid" response in receiving her divine message). He then openly invited the Lord to proceed with his message, while showing maximum receptivity—listening attentively with a readiness to obey and accept God's articulated will. Samuel uttered a "speaking" prayer that opened into a "listening" prayer—a paradigm on which to pattern our prayer life.

The problem is that very few souls engage habitually in listening prayer at all; even worse, even in their speaking prayer, it's more frequently a matter of chattering than of chatting—a kind of talking to God instead of talking *with* him. But prayer should be a dialogue, not a monologue! And in this dialogue, God has far more to say to us than we have to say to him. We usually don't give him a chance to have his say because we're poor listeners. The poet Emerson's advice, though paganized in its expression, is sound: "Let us be silent that we may hear the whispers of the gods."

THREE QUALITIES OF A GOOD LISTENER

Jesus said that his sheep *"listen* to his voice," *"know* his voice," and *"follow* him" (Jn 10:3-4). This implies that Jesus expects three things of those who claim to be his:

1. They *listen* to his voice attentively, not merely hearing it;

2. They *recognize* it clearly as his voice, thus discerning the communication as a divine message;

3. They *heed* his voice by lovingly accepting and obeying his will (see John 14:15, 21).

Since Jesus himself presents these three qualities as characteristics of those who are really his sheep, we might use them as a reliable checklist by which to calibrate our receptiveness to God's messages. Let us take a closer look at these three traits of a Christ-focused person.

1. **Listening.** Merely hearing something is not the same as listening to it. At this moment you may be hearing traffic sounds or birds chirping, but you are probably not listening to those sounds. Active listening requires both attention and interest—both of which admit of varying degrees. An opera buff can listen with rapt attention to operatic music for hours, while someone else would become bored in minutes. Likewise, a contemplative person might be enthralled with God-communicated insights for long periods, while one less spiritually mature might experience only ennui.

Obstacles to listening come every day from *within ourselves* (from limited attention span, lack of interest, faulty value system, distaste for what is heard, and so on), or from *outside ourselves* (from extraneous noise, or static or competing voices, for example). From a theological perspective, an example of the first category might be an attachment to sin that results in a spiritual hearing impairment: "They turn their ears away from the truth" (2 Tm 4:4). The second category includes distractions that come from the "noise" of the world (see 1 John 2:15), for "a friend of the [sin-defiled] world becomes an enemy of God" (Jas 4:4).

2. Recognizing. This implies familiarity with the Shepherd's voice as a result of hearing it frequently. It is far easier to recognize the telephone voice of a caller who phones you daily than one who calls only every year or two. But such recognition also implies that there is a clear *discernment* for knowing it is not a counterfeit communication from a trickster. An impersonator's voice is easily detected as fraudulent by one with close ties to the real friend. Jesus' true followers "will never follow a stranger; they will run away from him because they do not recognize a stranger's voice" (Jn 10:5).

The countless subtle allurements of the New Age movement are easily detected by a Spirit-filled person as fraudulent communication—not the voice of God. The lure of such things as astrology, reincarnation teaching, and various cults has no effect on the God-discerning individual. Also clearly seen as deceptive are the "fringe doctrines" vaunted by humanistically-tainted theologians and the watered-down, "demythologized" scripture presented by preachers and teachers (even some seminary teachers) in our times.

The Scriptures themselves warn us of such false teachers: "The Spirit clearly says that in later times some will abandon the faith and follow deceiving spirits and things taught by demons. Such teachings come through hypocritical liars, whose consciences have been seared" (1 Tm 4:1-2). In Paul's next letter to Timothy he elaborates on this: "The time will come when men will not put up with sound doctrine. Instead, to suit their own desires, they will gather around them a number of teachers to say what their itching ears want to hear. They will turn their ears away from the truth and turn aside to myths" (2 Tm 4:3-4). Paul minces no words about the importance of this discernment element for recognizing God's voice: "The man without the Spirit does not accept the things that come from the Spirit of God, for they are foolishness to him, and he cannot understand them, because they are spiritually discerned" (1 Cor 2:14).

3. Heeding. Heeding the voice of God is the ultimate criterion of the true follower of Christ. This characteristic is twofold. *Passive heeding* of God's voice is the loving acceptance of his providence in our lives—of everything from weather inclemencies to incurable cancer. It consists in the serene, love-filled acceptance of all the unalterable agonies as well as the delightful ecstasies of life. *Active heeding* of God's voice, on the other hand, is full-fledged obedience to his will in all things. It means to follow the shepherd, obeying all his directives, including those he gives to his sheep through his ecclesiastical shepherds (see Luke 10:16; Hebrews 13:17; 1 Thessalonians 5:12), who themselves should be "examples to the flock" (1 Pt 5:3).

Thus, heeding God's voice implies the faithful fulfilling of divine imperatives which may be given directly or indirectly. It means obeying a wide spectrum of injunctions, among them, tithing, not neglecting the sacrament of Confirmation, keeping the Church's laws on marriage and birth control, providing timely and proper sex education for children, frequently and devoutly receiving Holy Communion and the sacrament of Reconciliation. It may embrace such diverse things as the moral obligation to vote, generosity toward the poor, faithfulness in prayer and Scripture reading, prudent fasting, and the eschewing of the common sins of gluttony, gossip, lustful addictions, and rash judgment. The Lord's invitation is constant and comprehensive: "Give ear and come to me; hear me, that your soul may live" (Is 55:3).

THE CHALLENGE OF LISTENING TO GOD

For one not accustomed to it, any attempt at listening to the voice of God can seem quite burdensome. For the faith-filled person, however, it is quite the contrary. Like David, this person exclaims, "I delight in doing your will, O my God; your law is within my heart" (Ps 40:8). For any true child of God, each "heeding" is surcharged with joy-filled love. As St. John reminds us, "If anyone obeys his word, God's love is truly made complete in him" (1 Jn 2:5). Not only is there a love-filled joy now, but there is also an accumulated eternal reward to be enjoyed in the hereafter (see John 4:36). This Spirit-spawned joy exults with the chorus, "All this, and heaven too!"

Did you ever notice that those who complain most against God and his providence are those who do not heed his voice when he speaks? Three times the author of Hebrews quotes the warning from Psalm 95: "Today, if you hear his voice, do not harden your hearts." God told Zechariah how he dealt with the spiritually deaf: "When I called they did not listen, so when they called, I would not listen" (Zec 7:12-13).

Whether God is speaking to us through Scripture, his laws, our conscience, the example of others, inspirations of grace, life-events, "coincidences" or "near-misses," or any of a hundred and one other means, let us never neglect to tune in with our hearts and minds—to listen, recognize, and heed his voice.

Our very eternity may well be at stake.

SIXTEEN

Nestling in the Hand of God

A farmer watched a bird building its nest in a heap of branches pruned from an apple tree. Having planned to clear away that pile of branches soon, he destroyed the unfinished nest to discourage the bird from building there. Undaunted, the bird rebuilt her nest in the same spot. Again the farmer destroyed the nest. A third time the bird started to build its nest, but this time in a rose bush near the farmhouse. There, to the farmer's great delight and under his protective care, she later hatched her eggs and raised a brood of chicks.

Sometimes in life what is needed is not blind instinct but a long range view of particular situations. These are the times when the Lord, who sees the events of our life from a much better perspective than we do, often has to disrupt our plans in order to entice us to something better. God's over-arching plan for us his creatures is called providence, which means the act of providing, and which comes from the Latin *providere:* "to see before." This is reminiscent of Jesus' words to Peter,

"You do not realize now what I am doing, but later you will understand" (Jn 13:7).

The *Catechism of the Catholic Church* (#302) reminds us that creation "did not spring forth complete from the hands of the Creator. The universe was created in a state of journeying (*in statu viae*) toward an ultimate perfection yet to be attained, to which God has destined it." Divine providence encompasses "the dispositions by which God guides his creation toward this perfection." We are called to cooperate with God's plan, even when we cannot see its meaning as he does. Scripture reminds us: "Nothing in all creation is hidden from God's sight. Everything is uncovered and laid bare before the eyes of him to whom we must give account" (Heb 4:13).

THE HAND OF GOD IN THE GLOVE OF MAN'S FREE WILL

In view of this accountability, Vatican II says that God's providence includes "even those things which are yet to come into existence through the free action of creatures".[1] This leaves room not just for God's free will but also for our human free will to enter into the workings of divine providence. (This side-steps the depersonalized heresy which acknowledges only blind fate.)

For those with the highest sublimation of faith—the Holy Spirit's gift of wisdom (see Isaiah 11:2)—their involvement in divine providence bespeaks both an intimate *knowledge* or familiarity with God, and an *embracing* of this plan in their lives. In one sentence Solomon captured both of these elements: "Wisdom is *familiar* with God's mysteries and *helps determine* his course of action" (Wis 8:4). Again, this double dimension— our *belief* in God and his revealed truths and our *reliance* on his love-propelled plan for our welfare—is succinctly stated in 1 John 4:16: "We *know* and *rely* on the love God has for us." Thus, the two highest human faculties are engaged: the mind to *know* God and his revealed truth by belief, and the will to *rely* on his providential plan by exercising the virtue of trust.

This trust or reliance on God—the second aspect of true wisdom—is the soul's devout answer to God's holy will as articulated in his loving providence. Such devout surrender to God is the soul's way of saying, "I love you too, Lord." It is more than a mere tolerance of God's providential plan for us; it is a confident reliance on the *goodness* of God to work out his will for our best interests. Thus, with Jeremiah, we exult, "The Lord is *good* to those whose hope is in him" (Lam 3:25). In addition, our loving confidence in the Lord provides a divine thrill of joy for him, the psalmist tells us: "The Lord *delights* in those... who put their hope in his unfailing love" (Ps 147:11).

TRUSTING THE LORD—WHAT'S IN IT FOR ME?

To souls who rely on God, he bestows countless graces and blessings: "Blessed is the man who trusts in the Lord, whose confidence is in him" (Jer 17:7). A great reward is promised to those who consistently practice this trust: "Do not throw away your confidence; it will be *richly rewarded* (Heb 10:35). At least part of Zophar's advice to Job emphasized the security element of the reward, even in this life: "If you devote your heart to him and stretch out your hands to him... you will stand firm and without fear... You will be secure... and take your rest in safety" (Jb 11:13-17). The author of Proverbs restates this same advantage, but more succinctly: "Whoever trusts in the Lord is kept safe" (Prv 19:25).

But by his trust in Providence, the psalmist also expects a *future* eternal reward: "You hold me by my right hand. You guide me with your counsel, and afterward you will take me into glory.... My flesh and my heart may fail, but God is the strength of my heart and my portion forever" (Ps 73:23-26).

Those who master this virtue of trusting in God as a loving Father are never disappointed: "I am the Lord; those who hope in me will not be disappointed" (Is 49:23). And Paul adds, "Hope does not disappoint us, because God [the Father] has poured out his love into our hearts by the Holy Spirit" (Rom 5:5). And to complete the Trinitarian focus: "Such confidence as this is ours through Christ before God" (2 Cor 3:4). This never-disappointed confidence in the Godhead thus underlies the classic exhortation of the Epistle to the Hebrews: "Let us then approach the throne of grace with confidence" (Heb 4:16).

While God will never disappoint *us*, we may disappoint *him:* "I hold this against you: You have forsaken your first love" (Rv 2:4). Our love-animated trust must not be just a sporadic or passing feeling (such as a momentary spiritual "high" after a sermon on the subject). Like all virtues, it must be practiced consistently and perseveringly.

TRUSTING IN GOD: REHEARSAL FOR END TIME TRIALS

Persevering in loving trust will become critical in the coming end times—and surprisingly difficult in the anguish of the tribulation when God's loving concern will seem to have evanesced. Almost lamentably, Jesus asks a poignant question: "When the Son of Man comes, will he find faith on the earth?" (Lk 18:8). He will if Scripture's many encouragements on the subject are taken to heart. "Be faithful, even to the point of death, and I will give you the crown of life" (Rv 2:10). "You need to *persevere* so that when you have done the will of God, you will receive what he has promised" (Heb 10:35). "He who stands firm *to the end* will be saved" (Mt 10:22; 24:13).

Those who pridefully regard themselves as strong in their faith without humbly pleading for the grace of perseverance will find their faith—and hence their reliance on the Lord—failing in that critical time. In this regard, the words of Paul are sobering: "Be on your guard; stand firm in the faith" (1 Cor 16:13). "If you think you are standing firm, be careful that you don't fall!" (1 Cor 10:12).

But "now is the time of God's favor" (2 Cor 6:2); it is now—before the great tribulation—that we must cultivate a deeply formed *habit* (virtue) of trust in the Lord. No matter how great the trials ahead, our hearts must be able to cry out confidently with Job, "Though he slay me, yet will I hope in him" (Jb 13:15).

TRUST IN GOD: BATHTUB OF THE SOUL

Whether or not they admit it, every thinking adult, civilized or savage, has a consciousness of sin. This is the quasi-universal experience of guilt over the fact that "all have sinned and fall short of the glory of God" (Rom 3:23). It carries with it some intuitive dread of punishment or retribution. Both consciously and subconsciously, mankind has tried multifarious ways of dealing with real or imagined guilt.

Over the centuries, people have tried such varied approaches as self-flagellation, sleeping in coffins, submitting to ceremonial crucifixion, spending endless hours in self-focused meditation, and engaging in psychopathic masochism, or starvation-like fasting. None of these humanly engineered forms of erasing guilt has been found to be truly satisfactory. Only persons who rely on God's method of sin-dissolving, as delineated in both Old and New Testaments, have found success in this otherwise futile venture.

All sin, even that which offends our fellow humans, is ultimately an offense against God. It is a violation of his will as perceived, albeit inadequately, by the human conscience. Sin is therefore a rupture in a relationship between a rational (conscience-responsive) creature and his or her Creator. Restoring that disturbed *personal* relationship must involve not just the creature but also the offended Creator. Because this Creator is no impersonal cosmic "force" (not that we could relate to an impersonal or sub-personal entity anyway) this restoration must be carried out in a *personalistic* way. Fortunately for us, divine revelation shows us that our Creator is incredibly loving and far more eager to forgive us creatures than we are eager to be forgiven. And yet he requires us to be open to his proffered loving forgiveness; our willingness to accept his gift is an act of faith.

In this personalized dialogue, restoration of the relationship does not occur as the result of a meaningless and morbid remorse; rather, it results from a "godly sorrow [which] brings repentance that leads to salvation" (2 Cor 7:10). For Christians this is no abstract, meaningless exercise. The teaching of the New Testament provides healthy stimulants to genuine repentance as well as vivid depictions of God's mercy—in parables like the prodigal son, but especially in accounts of the very real, torturous passion and death of Jesus, the God who became the God-man, whose sufferings were designed by God himself as atonement for our sins.

All of this makes it consummately easy, even in a flashing moment, to be relieved of all guilt. No self-scourging or other self-imposed hardships are required. It is simply a matter of surrendering to God's forgiving love, which is made meaningful for us by the love-motivated sufferings of his Son Jesus. In this context, trust is the most beneficial act of personalized faith possible—it redounds to our very salvation.

How heartening to know that something so necessary—salvation—is something so easy. It simply means trusting God to manage our sins, just as we trust him to manage the supply of the air we breathe, the movement of atoms throughout the cosmos, or the rising of the sun. Of the thousands of possible ways in which we might attempt to attain true freedom from guilt and authentic peace, this is the *only* workable one: totally trusting the Lord to dissolve our sins in his merciful love, like tissue paper in a blast furnace. "If a wicked man turns away from all the sins he has committed and does what is just and right... none of the offenses he has committed will be charged against him.... Am I not pleased when they turn from their [wicked] ways?" (Ez 18:21-23). When our trust is a reliance on Christ's sin-atonement, we experience a Christic peace—one that transcends any ersatz worldly tranquillity: "*My* peace I give you... not as the world gives. Do not let your hearts be troubled" (Jn 14:27). But the moment we stop trusting Christ, we are left to drown in a sea of guilt.

BLESS THIS MESS

Less dangerous than outright sinning but perhaps even more common than sin for all of us is the daily failure rate we experience by simple mistakes. These range from tactless remarks to faulty stock market investments; from misspelled words to enough daily lapses in driving skills to make us flunk any driver's test; from checking account miscalculations to misplacing our glasses or the car keys. After my first hundred or so mistakes each morning, I smile at the acronym plaque on my desk that reads: "PBPWMGIFWMY"—"Please Be Patient With Me: God Isn't Finished With Me Yet."

With the psalmist, we must wonder what the faultless God really thinks of us in our failure-mottled lives. "What is man that you are mindful of him... that you care for him?" (Ps 8:4). But as another psalm affirms, and as Peter repeats, God really does care for us: "Cast all your anxiety on him, for he cares for you" (Ps 55:22; 1 Pt 5:7). Under the aegis of God's care, we must without anxiety truly trust him to help us blunder our way to heaven, where "failure" is not a word in the celestial vocabulary. But in the process of getting there, we can only *trust* that the Lord in his loving compassion will disregard all our missteps and exercise a kind of "damage control"—with the same mercy that drives him to disregard the sins we repented of.

Human reactions to failures and weaknesses will of course be as varied as human reactions to any other situations. Some people give hardly a thought to their daily imperfections and mistakes, with a so-what or a that's-the-way-I-am attitude.

Others take their missteps far too seriously and keep themselves in a fever of self-recrimination and self-vilification; they lose proper self-esteem, thinking that denying one's worth is only the way to holiness.

Finally, there are those mature souls who acknowledge their weaknesses and defects with true humility and then surrender them sweetly, lovingly, and peacefully into the hands of God, just as they trust him to keep their heart beating while they sleep. Such persons advance daily closer to God while avoiding the pitfalls of religious recklessness on the one hand and religious masochism on the other. The closer they come to God in holiness, the more keenly they perceive their unworthiness. But as the iron of their souls trustingly rests in the divine furnace of love, it grows from warm to hot to red hot and then white hot—penetrated ever more deeply with God's purifying love and holiness. They experience an ever deeper meaning in the words of Jesus, "Remain in me, and I will remain in you" (Jn 15:4).

If we have limitless trust in God, this seems to satisfy him as nothing else can do. That is because it corresponds to his eternal faithfulness and reliability, it honors his truthfulness, and it entails a silent, implicit worship of all his perfections. Not to rest in God is to derange the very plan of our creation. In St. Augustine's classic words: "Our hearts are made for thee, O Lord, and they cannot find rest until they rest in thee!"

PART IV

Shoulder to Shoulder in the Godward Trek

A steel mill worker in Gary, Indiana, made a dramatic bet with a group of fellow workers. He bet each one five dollars that he could harmlessly pass his naked finger through an inch-thick stream of molten iron pouring from a furnace. While they were covering his bet, he surreptitiously scooped up a handful of powdery dust from around the furnace, using it to blot the skin oil from his finger. He then whipped his dust-coated finger through the fiery stream of molten metal, painlessly scattering sparks as he did so. The wager won, he proceeded to collect his money from the amazed bettors.

One of them, who was unaware of the secret of the protective dust, decided to duplicate the feat himself. He set up a bet at another furnace down the line, with workers who hadn't seen the first demonstration. His unprotected finger was incinerated to the point where it had to be amputated.

Both good and evil consequences result from human activity that is based, consciously or otherwise, on imitation. Withholding truth or distorting it will have negative consequences on those around us; propagating truth will have positive consequences on them. Children acquire lifelong behavior patterns, prejudices, attitudes, and ideals by observing or imitating parents or teachers; politicians adopt policies by observing the successes or failures of their forerunners; scientists, musicians, engineers, and people in every field all learn from both their predecessors and their contemporaries. Society itself is fueled by countless forms of interpersonal influence.

In the spiritual life this personal interactivity ranges all the way from saintly edification to hell-inspired scandal. Fellow runners in life's marathon—and also curbside observers with their cheers or jeers—all leave an impacting influence on each of us as we strive to fulfill our God-designed destiny. Morally, the bottom line is that we are all co-responsible in some way for each other in striving for that destiny.

As we might expect, God's saving and sanctifying plan calls for cooperative love among his precious people. The psalmist exclaims of this love: "How good and pleasant it is when brothers live together in harmony!... For there the Lord bestows his blessing, even life forevermore" (Ps 133:1-3).

This last part of the book explores some of the ways that God blesses us with the input of others' love, as well as ways that he blesses us in our output of love toward others. This magnificent love dynamic demonstrates "the great and precious promises he has given us, so that through them you may *participate in the divine nature*" (2 Pt 1:4). We are thus caught up as participants into the cosmic orchestration of God's own love, for "God has poured out his love into our hearts by the Holy Spirit whom he has given us" (Rom 5:5). That Holy Spirit of love is Jesus-drawn from the bosom of our heavenly Father, "from whom his whole family in heaven and on earth derives its name" (Eph 3:15).

SEVENTEEN

Sharing the Lifeboat— The Meaning of Christian Fellowship

"To remove a thorn in one's foot, the whole body must bend over."

Zimbabwean proverb

This aphorism has provided generations of missionaries with an ideal analogy for teaching the Christian doctrine of the mystical body of Christ—that is, the interdependence of God's people who are related to one another by virtue of their union with Christ, the head of this body.

THE MEANING OF CHRISTIAN FELLOWSHIP

An arm or leg that has been amputated from the body and is no longer under the control of the head (the brain) is useless to the body's overall functioning. "Make every effort," says Paul, "to keep the *unity* of the Spirit through the bond of peace" (Eph 4:3). Connectedness is the first requirement for the awesome role of participating as a functioning member of Christ's mystical body. "No branch can bear fruit by itself; it must remain in the vine. Neither can you bear fruit unless you remain in me," warned Jesus, using another image to illustrate the same truth (Jn 15:4). Only when the soul is in union with Christ, the head and the vine, can it interact productively and efficiently with the entire corporate entity that we call Christ's mystical body.

As a baby grows and matures, his body parts move together in a more coordinated way; he stumbles less often and spills less food, managing to get less on his face and more into his mouth. Similarly, the degree to which we are spiritually coordinated (or co-active) with others is a measure of our maturity in Christ. Strive for this maturity, Paul urges, "that the body of Christ may be built up, until we all reach unity in faith and in the knowledge of the Son of God and become *mature,* attaining the whole measure of the *fullness of Christ*" (Eph 4:13).

Like a multifaceted gem, this doctrine of spiritual maturation in our relationship with others is iridescent with multiple aspects. There is the aspect of basic *unity* (which has ecumenical overtones for us)—a primary concern of Jesus himself (see John 10:16; 17:11, 20-23); the aspect of the virtues faith, hope and love among Christians (see Ephesians 4:2-5); the aspect of *mutual respect* (see Philippians 2:1-5) and *solidarity* (see 1 Corinthians 12:14-27; Romans 12:4-5); and above all the aspect of organic *union with Christ,* the vine (see John 15:4-5) and the head (see Eph 1:22-23; 4:12-16).

The pattern for this community of love is the union between the Father and the Son (see John 17:11, 22); its theological foundation is, of course, Scripture (see Ephesians 4:4-6; Galatians 3:27-28); and its historical model is the first apostolic community (see Acts 2:44; 4:32). The one dimension that I would like to highlight in this limited space is perhaps its most ignored dimension, namely, the altruistic thrust to which this doctrine of the mystical body insistently invites us.

PEOPLE NEED PEOPLE

"Just as the Son of Man did not come to be served but to serve" (Mt 20:28), so we are to "serve one another in love" (Gal 5:13). The New Testament writers never tire of exhorting us to this goal. After enumerating some of the ministry gifts given to various Christians, Paul says that these are to "prepare God's people for *works of service*" (Eph 4:12). And Peter adds a motivational note: "Each one should use whatever gift he has received to *serve* others, faithfully administering God's grace in its various forms.... He should do it with the strength God provides, so that in all things God may be praised through Jesus Christ" (1 Pt 4:10-11).

Hagiographies are replete with examples of the saints' successes in serving others in love. But some of our heroic contemporaries are no less successful—and unpretentious in their success as well. I heard of a man who asked a friend to help him repair his backed-up septic system. The friend cheerfully agreed, and after they had pumped the tank, he jumped into it to unclog the pipes. The owner looked down at him and asked, "Why are you down there doing the most distasteful part of the job, instead of me?" The friend, who had refused an enticing breakfast invitation for the same morning, answered that he had chosen to come because his help was needed.

Serving in love as a Christian entails a not-so-common spirit of cheerful and Christlike sacrifice. How many people do you know who would cheerfully forego an opportunity for a delightful outing in order to perform a distasteful task for a friend in need? More to the point, we might ask ourselves, "Am I one of those truly Christlike people?"

WE'RE IN THIS TOGETHER

Listen to a group of musicians in a pre-concert warm-up as they disregard each other's chords in a raucous cacophony; contrast that with the euphony of the concert music when the conductor coordinates the musicians' activity. So too the attempts of Christians to serve others must be orchestrated, not performed in a helter-skelter flurry of disconnected, individualistic activity. As Aaron and Hur worked *together to* hold Moses' hands lifted up in prayer until the Israelites vanquished the Amalekites (see Exodus 17:12), we too are called to a synergy of efforts in intercessory prayer and in evangelization, until the final victory (see 1 Chronicles 29:20; 1 Corinthians 3:6).

In crisis situations, sociologists have observed, this orchestration of functions comes about almost naturally; with survival at stake, it is easy to elicit people's cooperation and coordination of efforts. As one proverb puts it, "A friend loves at all times, but a brother is born for adversity" (Prv 17:17).

The Pearl Harbor attack galvanized Americans almost overnight into the most complex cooperative war effort that mankind had ever witnessed. Countless maritime disasters have proven that sharing a lifeboat in the face of threatened survival frequently (not always) elicits heroic cooperation—in bailing leaks, rationing food, subduing panic, and doing whatever else needs to be done.

Right now there is a crisis that calls for just such concerted, heroic activity. It is the threatened salvation of countless souls; in this ongoing crisis, which is greater than every other, we are called to cooperate with the Lord and with each other by our intercession and our zeal.

In May of 1960 a physicist captured the glare of a flash lamp using a rod of man-made ruby, which lined up what were usually scattered light waves; they were formed into the same length, put in step with each other, and focused in a single direction. This produced short bursts of red light that outshone even direct sunlight on the focused area. The result was one of the greatest breakthroughs in modern technology. Theodore Maiman had invented the LASER—an acronym for Light Amplification by Stimulated Emission of Radiation. According to Walter Oleksy in his book *Lasers,* a laser beam can deliver a *trillion* watts of power in a moment! That's the same amount of power that is used over the entire earth at any one time! The secret of such power is the synchronization of the light waves and the element of precise focus.

This analogy tells us something about the power of concerted action. Coordinating efforts in prayer and in service to others seemed quite natural to the early Christians. Luke writes that "they were filled with awe as many miracles and signs were done."

His next sentence may explain why so much power was being manifested: "All the believers were *together*" (Acts 2:43-44). They knew that Christians by definition are followers of Christ, who called himself the light of the world. They knew of his invitation: "Whoever follows me will never walk in darkness, but will have the light of life" (Jn 8:12). But later, after Christianity's honeymoon period, Jesus' followers neglected to follow Jesus that closely, and especially they neglected to follow him in real togetherness with each other. So John spelled out the communitarian corollary of Jesus' words about his power as Light of the world; in his first epistle he proclaimed, "If we walk in the light, as he is in the light, we have *fellowship* with one another" (1 Jn 1:7).

John recognized our tendency to live and work on "different wavelengths," out of step with each other. So he strove to "laserize" his readers—to incite them to worship together and to serve each other in holy fellowship.

Commenting on that passage in John, the biblical scholar B.F. Wescott proposes a sobering thought: Fellowship with the brethren is proof of fellowship with Christ; but if fellowship with him is lacking in your life, then you've missed your basic Christian calling, for "God has *called* you into fellowship with his Son Jesus" (1 Cor 1:9). Jesus clearly states that our relationship with him is contingent on our relationship with one another in spiritual endeavors: "Where two or three come together in my name, there am I with them" (Mt 18:20).

Even in Paul's time this pristine unity and cooperation were faltering. Like John, Paul felt constrained to "laserize" his contemporaries: *"Join with others,"* he wrote, "... take note of those who live according to the pattern we gave you" (Phil 3:17). He urged them to refocus on Jesus, who has "the power that enables him to bring everything under his control" (Phil 3:21). And even today in our own time, we're still not fully "laserized"—not synchronized with Christ. As both John and Paul explain, this is the main reason for the dissipation of spiritual and apostolic efforts, which are so often circumfused, like scattered light rays that are not yet focused and laserized. Jesus is the ruby that synchronizes and harmonizes our wavelengths.

Consider another analogy. Imagine an inflated balloon dotted with many small designs. As the balloon deflates, those markings come closer together; simultaneously, they all get closer to an imaginary point in the center of the air inside. As we get closer together in love of the brethren, we get closer to Christ, the center of our life. And in moving closer to him, we get closer to each other.

LOVE WITH ROLLED-UP SLEEVES

This Christocentric principle is not limited to fostering our *interior* spirituality by our mutual love in union with the Lord (see 1 John 2:10). It also brings new effectiveness to our *exterior* spirituality—to our zeal in the service of others and in building up the kingdom of God. By our respective ministries and our evangelistic endeavors we are all called to "make disciples of all nations" (Mt 28:19)—within the parameters of our God-given talents, gifts, and vocations, of course. In this exercise of zeal we can find supernatural support in the Lord's presence, for Jesus promised to be with us always in his Emmanuel ("God with us") role. After his ascension into heaven, *the Lord worked with them* [the disciples] and confirmed his word by signs" (Mk 16:20).

The Vatican II document, the *"Decree on the Apostolate of Lay*

People" (art. 10), urges the laity to follow "in the footsteps of the men and women who assisted Paul in his proclamation of the Gospel" (see Romans 16:1-16; Acts 18:18-26). When such persons exhibit truly earnest zeal for souls, it is a profound source of edification to others and a real consolation to pastors who come to depend on them more and more to reach so many who otherwise could not be reached.

The opportunities for lay involvement in loving service to others are almost limitless. Here are some examples:

- transporting invalids to church or to the doctor's office;
- becoming a children's catechist or lay evangelist, even in foreign missions;
- visiting sick or elderly parishioners in hospitals or convalescent homes (perhaps as a Eucharistic minister);
- getting involved in prison ministry (a highly rewarding service);
- baby-sitting for couples on a marriage retreat weekend;
- collecting food and clothing for the poor or working in a soup kitchen;
- making clothes for orphans or war-victim babies;
- being a hospital or Red Cross volunteer worker a few hours a week;
- teaching reading skills to the illiterate;
- preparing meals for bereaved families;
- spending a few hours a week taking a parish census or reaching fallen-away Catholics by the "doorbell ministry";
- working in ecological programs, pro-life activities, gang ministries, and "like-towards-like" organizations such as Alcoholics Anonymous or drug rehabilitation programs.

From the vast array of outreach choices one might select the most appropriate by a prayerful review of one's talents, interests, time, finances, vocation, and providentially fashioned circumstances.

The aforementioned decree on the laity puts special emphasis on the many lay ministries directed to one's own family, to youth, and to parish, diocesan, national and international endeavors. It emphasizes that "this life of intimate union with Christ in the Church is maintained by the spiritual helps common to all the faithful, chiefly by active participation in the liturgy" (art. 4).

ONE PLUS ONE IS NOT ALWAYS TWO

In God's mathematics, one plus one doesn't equal two; it equals the superabundance of the biblical "hundredfold." In plurality there is super-power. "Two are better than one, because they have a good return for their work" (Eccl 4:9). This is one of the first corollaries of the doctrine of the mystical body. We see this exemplified in petition prayer, where even the smallest possible group (two) exerts far more than twice the prayer power of one: "If two of you on earth agree about anything you ask for, it will be done for you" (Mt 18:19).

The same dynamic is operative in the exercise of the ministry of service; that's why Jesus sent his disciples out two by two instead of one by one to exercise their ministry of healing and exorcism (see Mark 6:7). Christians who cluster together to exercise their apostolates—in groups such as the Legion of Mary, for example—have proven to be more effective.

One of the most interesting examples of laypeople exercising their zeal for souls in a group situation is found in 1 Corinthians:

The household of Stephanas were the first converts in Achaia, and they have devoted themselves to the service of the saints. I urge you, brothers, to submit to such as these and to *everyone who joins in the work*, and labors at it. I was glad when Stephanas, Fortunatus and Achaicus arrived.... They refreshed my spirit and yours also. Such men deserve recognition.   1 Corinthians 16:15-18

In co-active group ministries or exercises of zeal, individual personal limitations are remarkably overcome by God's special providence. For instance, even the least educated persons ministering in Christ-centered fellowship can accomplish amazing evangelistic feats, like the ones the elders and teachers of the law witnessed in Jerusalem: "When they saw the courage of Peter and John and realized that they were unschooled, ordinary men, they were astonished" (Acts 4:13).

It is exciting to know that no matter who we are or what our background is, we are an important part of Jesus' mystical body; that as such we are called to help him build his Kingdom by drawing others closer to him by his own power surging through us. It is also exciting to realize that by loving Jesus in our fellow Christians we become more united with them in prayer and zeal, more able to effectively build with them following the magnificent design of the Divine Architect.

EIGHTEEN

Meekness Is Not Weakness

A rabbi and a cantor were rehearsing a service; at one point in the rehearsal, they fell on their knees as indicated, protesting, "I am nothing, I am nothing!" The janitor, following their example, did the same. Seeing this, the rabbi sneered, "Look who has the gall to think he's nothing!"

Mark Twain once quipped, "Modesty dies when false modesty is born." True modesty is rare but it is nonetheless an important characteristic of the wide-spectrumed virtue of meekness. We know this virtue best from Jesus' praise of it in the third beatitude: "Blessed are the meek, for they shall inherit the earth" (Mt 5:5). Some translations refer to meekness as "gentle spirit" (the *New English Bible*, for example) or, when it appears as a segment of the fruit of the Spirit, as "gentleness" (Gal 5:23). Whatever word may be used, however, it is a feeble translation for a virtue that is really a multiple concept and has no adequate one-word translation. Perhaps the best definition of meekness is the compound description from James: "The wisdom that comes from heaven is first pure; then peace-loving, considerate, submissive, full of mercy and good fruit, impartial and sincere" (Jas 3:17).

Words shift in meaning as languages evolve. In Old English, "girl" used to mean a young person of either sex, a "harlot" was simply a fellow, "lewdness" meant ignorance, and "villain" meant farm worker. In Shakespeare's time, "nice" meant foolish and "rheumatism" meant head cold. Today "meek" evokes an image of a Walter Mitty or Casper Milquetoast character, a somewhat spineless nerd. But that is not its original meaning.

To truly understand the third beatitude, it is imperative that we explore the *original* meaning of the words which our Bibles usually translate as "meek." This requires looking at both the New Testament Greek word and also the Old Testament Hebrew word, since the third beatitude quotes from Psalm 37:11: "The meek will inherit the land."

The Hebrew word *anaw* is translated as humble, lowly, or meek (a favorite word in Psalms, Proverbs and Isaiah). It describes a person who, in loving, obedient humility and without resentment or bitterness, always accepts God's guidance and providence as the best way. Such a one is dear to God, grace-filled and joy-filled, a person whose undemanding prayers are heard by God, and who is uplifted, defended, and saved.

Anaw emphasizes a person's "vertical" relationship to God. The Greek word *praus,* on the other hand, emphasizes one's "horizontal" relationship to *others.* Growth in meekness ideally starts with the "vertical" and melts into the "horizontal." Just as an ice cube becomes more "horizontal" as it melts into water, so also meekness remains the same virtue when it finds its expression in human relationships. For instance, meekly submitting to providentially designed, God-permitted hardships and sufferings produces a kind of tranquil joy. This kind of response is also the first step toward the mastery of a meekness response to harassments from fellow humans—discourteous drivers, irksome fellow-workers, nagging spouses, lazy associates, slow waiters, noisy neighbors, and so on.

The Greek word *praus,* with its rich connotations, corresponds to the Latin *mitis,* which is used to describe an animal that has been tamed or domesticated, like a sheep dog or seeing-eye dog; the creature is no longer wild but "under control."

Another example of strength under control is a carpenter driving a nail into a board. Without control, he might miss the nail altogether or, "hit the nail on the finger." In behavioral situations, what would otherwise be violent anger or out-of-control strength is tamed by the virtue of meekness.

Aristotle taught that "virtue is in the middle ground," (*"virtus stat in medio"*), so in his *Nicomachean Ethics* he says that anyone who is *praus,* or meek, possesses a self-controlled (tamed) emotional quality that lies midway between anger and apathy. Such persons exert their anger only for the right reason, in the right manner, against the right persons, at the right moment, for the right length of time. They are tranquil and stable, yet not too slow-tempered or apathetic. They can easily bear reproaches and slights, are not easily provoked, bitter or argumentative. They act with gentleness even when they have the authority to act sternly.

In leadership circumstances, true meekness patterns itself after the Christian concept of authority, which forbids lording it over others. "Whoever wants to become great among you must be your servant" (Mt 20:26; see 1 Peter 5:3). Jesus, "though he was in the form of God... emptied himself, taking the form of a servant" (Phil 2:6-7). True meekness is "gentle giant" meekness. To use Browning's dictum, "It is good to have a giant's strength, but it is tyrannous to use it like a giant."

As its classical meaning shows—and in contrast to our modern understanding—meekness is not weakness. Neither is it indifference or fear-engendered gentleness or unprincipled tolerance. (Charles Dickens' character, Uriah Heep, comes to mind.) It is, like the ancient Greek historian Xenophon's description of the Persian king Cyrus' virtue, "gentleness with commanding presence."

The horizontal, or other-oriented, aspect of the Greek word *praus* is exemplified by the attitude urged by Paul: "Be angry but do not sin" (Eph 4:26, RSV). Anger for our own sake is sinful; for the sake of others, it is often divinely right. Jesus was never angry at the insults, injuries, or slights that he himself received; but he angrily denounced the Scribes and Pharisees for giving precedence to observing details of the Sabbath law instead of to alleviating human suffering (see the account of his healing the man with a withered hand in the ʾhird chapter of Mark, for example).

Jesus also denounced disrespect for the sacred precincts of the temple (see John 2:16). All four gospels record the Chrʾst of love becoming the Christ of the whip when he saw money changers making iniquitous profit out of poor pilgrims in the temple court, and the temple itself thus misused. Jesus' selfless anger blazed—and this immediately after his meek processional arrival, *"gentle* and riding on a donkey" (Mt 21:5). His just indignation was altruistic: it was an act of "zeal for his Father's house" and protection of the greed-victimized pilgrims from the money-changers. His anger was meek because it was saving, not destructive; healing, not lacerating.

The indignation of a reformer is not a selfish indignation but a selfless one, and it is effective because it is tamed or controlled. "For God did not give us a spirit of timidity, but a spirit of power, of love and of self-discipline" (2 Tm 1:7).

Like Jesus, Paul knew a meekness that could be either strong or pliant, depending on the circumstances. To the unruly Christians in Corinth he presented the options: "What do you prefer? Shall I come to you with a whip, or in love and with a gentle spirit?" (1 Cor 4:20). Without sacrificing the virtue of meekness, he could be firm and uncompromising when necessary, for he well understood that to be meek is not to be weak.

What can help us to decide whether to respond with gentleness or firmness in a given situation? Three principles might offer some guidance here:

1. *When our own rights are at stake, it is usually appropriate to be accommodating*—to yield our self-will to the demands of others, except in criminal matters. We are urged to "turn the

other cheek," to be vulnerable to repeated insults or rejection (but not injury).

But when it is God's right that is at stake, or the rights of others, then the situation may require a more aggressive approach. Still, love and suavity are called for, not harshness; and the anger must be directed against the injustice, not the culprit (see Jude 23). While hating the sin we must love the sinner, as St. Augustine says, so that we can "be angry and sin not" (Eph 4:26).

2. *If the situation is within the ambit of our authority, as a father making family decisions, firmness may be required where gentle persuasion is unavailing.* If the situation is outside our range of authority, we may have to limit the pressure to suggestions or some similar approach.

3. *Consummate prudence must be employed,* with prayerful consideration of what would be the most helpful approach in the circumstances. Pray for the prudence which is sublimated by the gift of the Holy Spirit, known as the gift of counsel (see Isaiah 11:2).

NO MEEK-END HOLIDAYS

Hardly a day passes—or even an hour—in which we are not challenged to practice the meekness that Jesus enjoins in the third beatitude. Living out the basic Godward (or vertical) aspect of meekness—the *primary* meaning found in Scripture—requires that we acknowledge our own inadequacy and therefore our need for dependence on God for guidance. But this in turn spills over into the horizontal dimension, into all aspects of human interaction: social encounters, conflicts, challenges, tense relationships, hurts, and hardships. Among the earmarks of the meek in this horizontal dimension:

1. *In social encounters a meek person shows consummate respect for others*—a refined form of courtesy avoiding both arrogance and aloofness: "Be peaceable and considerate and show true humility toward all" (Ti 3:2).

2. *In potential conflict, the meek have the strength to sidestep unnecessary confrontation.* "The Lord's servant must not quarrel; instead he must be kind [meek] to everyone" (2 Tm 2:24). Jesus reprimanded his apostles for wanting to call down fire from heaven on the inhospitable Samaritans (see Luke 9:54-55).

3. *In facing challenges, the meek reflect the attitude of Mary:* "Behold the handmaid of the Lord; be it done to me according to your word" (Lk 1:38). Meekness motivated Paul's compliance to God's command to go into the city (see Acts 9:6).

4. *In tense human relationships, the meek pattern their response after that of Jesus.* He made it easy for embarrassed Peter to reconcile with him after a triple denial, gently offering a triple opportunity to reinstate his love (see John 21:15-17) and then trusting him to care for his followers, his lambs and sheep. "A bruised reed he will not break, and a smoldering wick he will not snuff out" (Is 42:3).

5. *In personal hurts, the meek strive to imitate the gentle Jesus* who, when mocked, spat upon, and crucified, responded only with "Father, forgive them..." Peter reminds us of Jesus' meekness: "When they hurled insults at him, he did not retaliate; when he suffered, he made no threats. Instead, he entrusted himself to him who judges justly" (1 Pt 2:23).

6. *In hardship, the meek manifest the attitude of Job:* "The Lord gave and the Lord has taken away" and "Though he slay me, yet I will trust him" (Jb 1:21; 13:15). In suffering, the

strength of the meek mirrors Jesus' heroic, voluntary, magnanimous, and trustful surrender to this Father's will: "Father, not as I will, but as you will" (Mt 26:39).

STRENGTH IN MEEKNESS

More than once I've been surprised to find cats and dogs living peacefully together in the same home. And some people might be surprised to learn that the meekness and assertiveness can thrive side by side in the same person, as different aspects of the same virtue. To understand how it is possible to be assertive and meek at the same time, take a close look at the meek-but-not-weak behavior of Jesus before the high priest:

> The high priest questioned Jesus about his disciples and his teaching. "I have spoken openly to the world," Jesus replied. "I have always taught in the synagogues or at the temple where all the Jews come together. I said nothing in secret. Why question me? Ask those who heard me. Surely they know what I said."
>
> When Jesus said this, one of the officials nearby struck him in the face. "Is this the way you answer the high priest?" he demanded.
>
> "If I have said something wrong," Jesus replied, "testify as to what is wrong. But if I spoke the truth, why did you strike me?"   **John 18:19-23**

Jesus had the courage to answer openly but did not allow the high priest to put him on the defensive about his teachings. When he was slapped, Jesus replied in a nonviolent way to the injustice. He showed that meekness is clearly not weakness, but a God-controlled strength. His example illustrated his divine pedagogy: "Learn of me, for I am meek and humble of heart" (Mt 11:29).

An incident in the life of Gandhi illustrates the strength of meekness. As he led the Indians in a protest against the unfair salt laws, the British soldiers clubbed the first line of protesters to the ground. Successive waves of protesters stepped forward and suffered the same fate. The British soldiers finally were compelled to stop their violence in the face of such inner strength. By meekness, the Indians became victorious.

There is a power in meekness that the violent cannot understand. The author of Proverbs phrased it adroitly: "When a man's ways are pleasing to the Lord he makes even his enemies live at peace with him" (Prv 16:7).

HOLY MOSES

Moses was called meek—"more than anyone else on the face of the earth" (Nm 12:3). But Moses had to be tamed into this meekness while hiding for forty years as a desert hermit, after impetuously killing an Egyptian. Called to lead God's people, he meekly demurred as unworthy, yet he could blaze forth in righteous anger against the rebelliousness of his followers. He meekly accepted rejection by his sister Miriam and his brother Aaron for marrying an Ethiopian woman, but when God punished Miriam with leprosy, Moses meekly begged God to heal her (see Numbers 12:1, 13).

Moses had learned that a meek person exerts God's strength, not his own, when he does not flinch at criticism from others nor seek revenge: "It is God who arms me with strength and makes my way perfect" (Ps 18:32). He was aware that "the steps of a good man are ordered *by the Lord*" (Prv 16:9) and that "it is not for man to direct his own steps" (Jer 10:23).

Yet even the world's greatest champion of meekness failed to exercise it consistently: at Meribah, "rash words came from Moses' lips" against the rebellious Israelites (Ps 106:33). For this failure in meekness, Moses was forbidden to enter the promised land; he was only allowed to view it across the Jordan from Mount Pisgah. But since Moses took this crushing disappointment with consummate meekness, his faith in God was strengthened by it, not shattered. Despite his failures, the great qualities of meekness shine forth in Moses: absolute trust in God and reliance on his great wisdom and mercy.

Often-heard graveside advice affirms that "God is too wise to ever make a mistake and too loving to ever be unkind." If we could really come to grips with those words, we would catch some of the spirit of meekness that Moses exemplified. Rather than rebelling against Providence-designed adversity, we would be lovingly content—even thrilled—to accept the "Mount Pisgah experience" of disappointment, blindly and lovingly affirming that "he whose walk is blameless... will never be shaken" (Ps 15:2-5). And we would remember that "in all things God works for the good of those who love him" (Rom 8:28). Such meekness is not a mere passive acceptance but embodies a fully ripe fruit of the Spirit, joy. "The meek will *rejoice* in the Lord" (Is 29:19).

WHERE THERE'S A WILL...

Where Moses failed to enter into the promised land, Caleb succeeded. He exemplifies the five kinds of people described in Psalm 37, who will "inherit the land": "the meek," "those who hope in the Lord," "those the Lord blesses," "the righteous," and "those who wait for the Lord and keep his way" (Ps 37:11, 9, 22, 29, 34).

All these meekness qualities were found in Caleb, the only non-rebel among the children of Israel—and the only one except Joshua from the *original* exodus populace that entered the Promised Land (thousands were born en route during the forty years). God said, "Caleb has a different spirit and *follows me wholeheartedly.* I will bring him into the land he went to, and his descendants will inherit it" (Nm 14:24).

This brings us to the other linchpin in this third beatitude, along with the word "meek": "inherit." (This very word creates a paradox: the meek are not losers but winners in God's game-plan.) "Blessed are the meek, for they shall inherit the earth." For us, inheriting usually means receiving something which has been left to us, bequeathed in a will. In Scripture, though, inheriting often implies receiving something promised and foretold by God.

But what does it mean to "inherit the *earth*"? The *Jerusalem Bible* says, "They shall have the earth for their inheritance." The *New American Bible* says, "They will inherit the land." The *New English Bible* says, "They shall have the earth for their possession." "Earth" or "land"—what does it signify?

The early Jews who read Psalm 37 interpreted it as the land promised to the children of Israel (Palestine). Later they took it to mean the kingdom of God on earth during the coming age of the Messiah. Christians of apostolic times probably took it to mean the promise of life here and now while we are on earth, with two special characteristics as reward: peace and power.

"The meek will inherit the earth and enjoy *great peace*" (Ps 37:11). The person who has committed himself and his life to the Lord has the gift of peace that Jesus promised—peace that the world cannot give (see John 14:27) or ever take away, for nothing can separate him from the love of God (see Romans 8:39). Even in earlier times the Lord had promised, "If you follow my decrees and obey my commands [the first characteristic of meekness]... I will grant *peace* in the land, and you will lie down and no one will make you afraid" (Lv 26:3-6). How blessed the heirs of such a land—free from fear of injury, theft, rape, crime, gang attack, and everything else that puts peace to flight.

The meek will experience *power*—again showing that meekness is not weakness. They exert the power of social influence through persuasion, example, and leadership. Theirs too is the power of self-discipline through mastery of anger and passion. Only those who rule themselves can rightly rule others.

Moreover, besides this social power, the meek are also given physical power over nature. The power over the earth (material reality) that is inherited by the meek is a share in God's power over the earth, which Paul refers to in Romans 1:20. God shares with his gentle, lowly, meek children his miracle and healing power over his material creation—the same God-derived power that Moses exercised in effecting his astonishing miracles.

The people who "inherit the land" in peace and power are not those who are merely "self-controlled"—for complete self-control is beyond human power, as experience shows. They are those who are God-controlled. "Only the mind controlled by the Spirit is life [power] and peace" (Rom 8:6).

A WEAKNESS THAT NEEDS MEEKNESS

Today the virtue of Christian meekness is fast becoming an unknown behavior response. Current statistics regarding home violence show a truly alarming increase, especially in wife and child abuse. Physical, verbal, emotional, and sexual abuse of children has become a major social sickness—abortion being the worst of its forms. Ninety-five percent of all prostitutes were victims of incest as children. The same percentage of male convicts were mentally or physically abused in the home. A boy with an abusive father and victimized mother frequently becomes an abusive husband and father himself. Today as never before, there is a desperate need for God-centered meekness to be cultivated in our society.

Plutarch once asked how a fig tree, whose branches, stems, roots, and leaves are so bitter, could bear such sweet and pleasant fruit. We might well ask how the sweet fruit of the Spirit— gentleness or meekness—can grow on the bitter stock of human nature. As Joyce Kilmer wrote in his well-known poem, "Only God can make a tree," only he can make sweet the fruit on that tree. Those who come before the Lord in the meekness of Moses and live in imitation of Jesus, who was eminently "meek and humble of heart," will bear in their lives the sweet fruit of Godlike meekness.

This sweet fruit of the Spirit softens the harshness of life, as a carpet deadens a floor creak or as a curtain holds off a winter wind. It is a pillow that halves the pain in sickness. It conveys tenderness, affection, gentleness, and love to a world that needs buffering from the acrid fumes of hedonism, selfishness, greed, and conflict.

We might paraphrase the third beatitude as follows: "Oh the blessedness, the happiness, of the God-committed, God-controlled persons, whose God-derived, tranquil and gentle strength binds them in loving relationship with others, for they will inherit that fullness of life that God has promised to such precious ones."

NINETEEN

The Poison of Bad Example

The operator of a factory whistle made sure to synchronize his watch daily with a local crony who was famous for keeping exact time with his digital watch. One day the whistle operator asked the old man how he always knew the exact time.

"Oh that's easy," the man replied. "Every day I set my watch by the sound of the factory whistle."

In life we never know who might be setting his watch by ours. Sardonic wags may dismiss our ensuing responsibility with quips such as, "None of us is entirely useless. Even the worst of us can serve as bad examples." But few people really want to be among "the worst"—passing through life leaving a noxious exhaust of toxic fumes: broken hearts, anger, misery, and sin. Most of us aspire to be among those who, comet-like, leave a sparkling trail of love, joy, and peace in our wake, lighting a candle now and then in this sin-darkened world. In the back of our minds, though, we acknowledge the possibility that hell's worst suffering may be viewing the harm we have done to others during life.

Since we are interwoven as "God's one family in heaven and on earth" (Eph 3:15), our interdependence may be such that every action of our life touches some chord that will resonate in the souls of others for eternity. Pope John XXIII ventured to suggest that we are saved and sanctified in clusters, like grapes. Perhaps we are damned the same way—adulterous partners together, Mafia brotherhoods together, and so on. This is at least one possible conjecture flowing from Jesus' words of warning: "Things that cause others to sin are bound to come, but woe to that person by whom they come" (Lk 17:1; Mt 18:7). Perhaps we should be even more concerned with not being bad examples than with lifting the bushel to let our light of good example shine before men.

History shows that the far-reaching effects of bad example can hardly be overestimated. Thousands of youth adopted the tattoo slogan, "Born to raise hell," in imitation of the tattoo worn by a serial killer in Chicago some years ago. The bloody deeds described in Homer's classic, *The Iliad,* influenced Alexander the Great to emulate them—which in turn morbidly influenced Caesar, Sweden's Charles XII, and later the Turkish Emperor Selymus in his merciless wars in Egypt and Persia. The blind poet Homer never knew what torrent of evil would flow from his enchanting poem. The American crime novel, *The Snatchers,* provided the ingenious plan for the kidnapping of the auto magnate Eric Peugeot in France.

One frightening aspect of our less than perfect behavior is the fact that we never know who might be walking in our shadow. People whose character is not autonomously formed will tend to let others form it for them. But when the blind lead the blind, Jesus reminds us, both can fall into the ditch; that doubles the hazard. Since there will always be people who "set their watch" according to ours, it is essential to cultivate a sense of responsibility for others—at least as one motive for virtue—and to synchronize our watches with the objective norm of Christian morality and virtue. A single act of ours may turn the tide of another's life—either way. There's always someone around with a head like a doorknob: anyone can turn it. That fact alone might entice us to adopt as our own the anonymous prayer-poem:

> My life shall touch a dozen lives before the day is done;
> Leaving marks of good or ill, e'er sets the evening sun.
> This, the wish I always wish, the prayer I always pray:
> Lord, let my life help others' lives
>   that cross my path this day.

We might also take a serious inventory of our behavior periodically. After all, we can't induce others to upgrade their lives to a level higher than our own. To really impact others for good, we must become saints in shoe leather, not stained glass. Ideals that are lived out are the only ones that really count. We must come down from the bleachers and get onto the playing field. In doing this, we must master that delicate art of humbly pursuing holiness while letting our light shine before others— and in such a way that not we but our "heavenly Father may be glorified" (Mt 5:16).

THE DANGER OF "EASY ETHICS"

As we examine our own behavior, keep in mind that we have more need to focus on the danger of bad example than on the advantages of good example. The affirmation we receive through others' compliments usually make us quite conscious of whatever good example we may be setting. But our bad example we tend to rationalize away: "Everybody cheats on their income tax"; "premarital sex is OK if you love the person"; "motel prices are raised to cover the cost of these stolen towels"; "I don't have to treat her kindly since she rebuffed me."

We tend to downplay the effects of bad example, especially on children, who are particularly vulnerable to it. A TV jester's one-liner expressed it with a twist: "More kids would follow in their parents' footsteps if they weren't afraid of getting caught."

Often copy-cat behavior patterns are perpetuated transgenerationally. Three-fourths of youngsters from broken homes will end their own marriages in divorce, and 90 percent of them never fully recover psychologically from the trauma of their parents' divorce. Sixty-five percent of drug or alcohol dependent youths have at least one parent who is also hooked. Parental bad example can leave a cursed legacy for the offspring.

But all across the board, behavior is contagious, as every sociologist knows. Traffic flow tests have revealed that each driver in a line of cars approaching a stop sign will tend to follow the example of the driver in front of him in making a complete or an incomplete stop. Example exerts its power—sometimes subconsciously—by a kind of social osmosis. Of course the consequences are more far-reaching when the paradigmatic behavior has moral, not just legal, overtones. (Witness adolescent cluster suicides following a celebrity suicide.)

The ominous caveat of Jesus—"Woe to those who cause others to sin"—should be emblazoned on the mind of anyone contemplating marital infidelity, homosexual practices, unethical business deals, shoplifting, lying, harboring resentment, and other such behavior. Such activities extend their ill effects out to others, either engaging them as conspirators or, at the least, encouraging them to lower their own moral standards imperceptibly.

Some of this deadly influence is slow and subtle. Like the frog that quickly jumps out of scalding water but will allow itself to be boiled to death in slowly heated water, many people are killed spiritually over a period of time by witnessing or imitating the bad example of those around them.

This pernicious gradualism is often found in persons who have developed permissive attitudes about the outrageous atrocity of abortion. How can one measure the bad example of those who legislate, encourage, permit, or perform the killing of a million and a half unborn babies every year in the US—a genocidal crime that cries to God for vengeance? The bloody bodies of these "holy innocents" presented as evidence in the divine court of justice will expose the twisted thinking of those who feel that "if it's not illegal, it's not immoral"—a fallacy gradually incorporated into the mindset of millions who have been exposed to the example of countless abortions.

Warped reasoning also champions "safe" abortions, ignoring the fact that no abortion is "safe" for the child. It propagates the sophism that "a woman has a right to her own body"—while disregarding the right to life of the child within her. When such distorted thinking is articulated often enough, it has an inevitable influence on many people. Most affected are those whose moral opinions have not yet crystallized into convictions, especially young people who are subjected to this pervasive, deleterious propaganda. (One recalls that Communist indoctrination techniques made effective use of this pedagogical approach.)

Jesus reserved his strongest excoriation for such Pied Piper seducers. Better for anyone to be drowned with a millstone necklace than to cause one of these "little ones" to sin (see Luke 17:2; Matthew 18:6)! Such chastisement apparently extended to infractions far less serious than child molestation—possibly to such scandals as neglect of good training (see Proverbs 22:6; 29:15), neglect of a prayerful home life (see Isaiah 38:19), and neglect of church attendance (see Hebrews 10:25). David failed to restrain his son Adonijah (see 1 Kings 1:6), as Eli failed to restrain his sons (see 1 Samuel 3:13), and both reaped prolonged punishment from God. As the pithy Dutch proverb has it: "To teach youth nothing is to teach them evil."

Scandals are bound to happen, Jesus warns, but "woe to anyone by whom they come" (Lk 17:1). The certainty of scandal does not exculpate the scandal-giver. The inevitable downscaling of our societal mores through the ubiquitous, compelling influence of today's movies and TV programs burdens the entertainment moguls with a fathomless responsibility before God. The all-pervasive media has portrayed virulent evil—fornication, adultery, homosexuality, and the like—as almost normal, or at least not too unacceptable, "appealing to the lustful desires of sinful human nature" (2 Pt 2:18). Our threshold of tolerance of such behavior ratchets lower each year. But Jesus' prediction reminds us that just as the scandal is inevitable, so is its cost: someone is going to pay for the damage. "Woe to anyone..." is not an empty threat from our patient-but-outraged God.

Ecologists remind us that all of us, even the best intentioned, are environmental polluters. This is true of moral pollution too. Just as we need repeated reminders about littering, recycling, emissions testing and so on, we also need to be reminded that a little bad example can be far-reaching and destructive. (In 1 Corinthians and Romans, Paul teaches that even acceptable behavior should be avoided if it scandalizes anyone with an unformed conscience.)

Just as an oil spill has tragic effects far beyond the coastline it contaminates, one person's actions can have far-reaching and overwhelming consequences for others. Referring to the sexual immorality of only one person in the Corinthian community, Paul asks, "Don't you know that only a little yeast works through the whole batch of dough?" (1 Cor 5:6). Ecclesiastes employs another image: "As a dead fly can give perfume a bad smell, so a *little* folly outweighs wisdom and honor." (Eccl 10:1). And using another metaphor, the author of the Song of Songs emphasizes that "it is the *little* foxes that ruin the vineyard" (Sg 2:15). The least significant person or the least significant act can do widespread harm—or good.

The most efficacious tool for maintaining our own moral uplift is prayerful reading of God's Word (see Psalm 119:9). And as we experience the personal moral and spiritual "upgrading" that results, we also grow in our sense of responsibility to those who are treading in our footsteps. For whether we are aware of it or not, it is most likely that someone is watching and imitating us, in however subtle a way. We must let ourselves be imitated without being intimidated by this awesome responsibility of avoiding scandal. We will succeed in this insofar as we try to live by the great dictum of Paul: "In everything set an example by doing what is good" (Ti 2:7).

TWENTY

When Loved Ones Turn from God

*"The music was nice," the little girl told the
pastor just after the church service had ended.
"But the commercial was too long."*

Boredom at church services is not uncommon and is certainly not a sin—though it is certainly not the ideal. But when boredom—or any other reason, for that matter—causes people to stop attending church or to attend only rarely, then it becomes alarming. The Word of God warns us not to neglect church meetings, "as some are in the habit of doing" (Heb 10:25).

This neglect often marks the beginning of a downhill slide that puts many a Christian on a path of spiritual deterioration. It was to such persons that Paul must have been writing when he warned: "If you think you are standing firm, be careful that you don't fall"—adding a word of encouragement for those who recognize their danger: "but when you are tempted, God will also provide a way out so that you can stand up under it" (1 Cor 10:12-13). This "way out" frequently comes through the fervent intercessory prayers of a devout family member with a worrisome concern for such "unchurched" fallen-aways.

It is hard to find a Christian family today that does not have one or more black sheep who have given up church attendance, or perhaps even basic morality, and turned away from God. If you are distraught by such a sad situation in your family, be assured that the situation is not hopeless; you need not be frustrated when your prayers seem unanswered.

Your anguish at seeing your loved ones drift away from the Lord is a common suffering experienced by those who strive to love the Lord in these tumultuous and dissolute times. The coldness and indifference of your loved ones wound the heart of Jesus more than they can ever imagine—infinitely more than it hurts you. But the "burden" you have for them reflects your zeal for their spiritual welfare. This special grace God has given you carries with it a certain responsibility—and privilege—to intercede for them with fervent and persevering prayer.

If you want to intercede effectively, you must start with yourself. When the evangelist Gypsy Smith was asked how to start a spiritual revival, he gave this answer: "Go home, lock yourself in your room, and kneel down in the middle of the floor. Draw a chalk mark around yourself, and ask God to start a revival inside that chalk circle. When he has answered your prayer, the revival will be on its way."

R.A. Torrey's suggestion was similar: "Get a few Christians who are close to God to bind themselves together in prayer and put themselves at the disposal of God. This is sure to bring conversions. I have given this prescription around the world and have never seen it fail." To bring back lost sheep, God needs not just intercessors, but truly holy intercessors: "The prayer of a *righteous* man is *powerful and effective*" (Jas 5:16).

The distressing "prodigal" problem can be approached in several ways, among them: by reviewing the need for intercessory prayer ("standing in the gap"), by showing the importance of faith and hope, by urging perseverance. But here I wish simply to point out a few guidelines for making prayer effective in converting prodigals. Most of these norms derive from the story of the prophet Jonah.

1. *Pray that Divine Providence use the hurtful consequences of sinners' rebellion to draw them to himself.* Every choice we make produces consequences that are either good or bad, depending on whether or not the choice is according to God's purpose. Those who love God do his will (see John 14:15), and it is therefore only "for those who love him" that "all things work together for good" (Rom 8:28). But if the choice is contrary to God's will, the effects can sometimes be hurtful situations by which God often tries to pressure the rebellious soul to return to him.

Jonah, ignoring God's call to go east to convert Nineveh, sailed west instead "to flee the Lord" (Jon 1:3). God "pursued" him to persuade and even pressure him with hardships to follow his divine plan, without of course interfering with the function of Jonah's free will.

Prodigals seem to have "blinded eyes and deadened hearts" (Jn 12:40; see Isaiah 6:10). Or, as Paul says, "The god of this age [the devil] has blinded the minds of unbelievers, so that they cannot see the light of the gospel" (2 Cor 4:4). Jesus provided the light of the gospel, so the problem is not the lack of light but faulty vision: "when your eyes are bad, your whole being is full of darkness" (Lk 11:34). After establishing himself as a witness "greater than Jonah," Jesus said, "I have come into this world as a light, so that no one who believes in me should stay in the darkness" (Jn 12:40). Yet he reminds us that light enlightens only those who are *near* it (see Luke 11:36).

Some prodigals are *very* far from that light, others less distant. Paul describes those farthest away as "darkened in their understanding and separated from the life of God because of the ignorance... due to the hardening of their hearts. Having lost all sensitivity, they have given themselves over to sensuality and indulge in every kind of impurity with a continual lust for more" (Eph 4:18-20).

Blinded by this interior darkness, some sinners need time to experience and see the sour fruit of their rebellion. Even Jonah only belatedly recognized that his sin had brought about the life-threatening storm at sea (see Jonah 1:12) and was the reason he was thrown overboard and swallowed by the great fish. It may take years for some prodigals to recognize that their various trials—marriage failures, domestic problems, sickness, financial worries, unemployment, depression, their children's recalcitrance—are God-permitted pressures or forms of discipline inviting them to repent (see Hebrews 12:10-11).

While charitably providing help for suffering prodigals, intercessors should pray that such divinely engineered discipline will be effective in converting them, patiently allowing for God's timing. In a few cases, repentance may occur only as a last-minute deathbed conversion.

Furthermore, both sinners and those who pray for them should remember that even when repentance is prompt, the adverse effects of sin may linger. David showed immediate remorse when confronted with his sin of engineering Uriah's death, but he did not escape the consequences: his baby (and later, three sons) experienced tragic deaths, and peace left his house—"The Lord said, 'Out of your own household I am going to bring calamity upon you'" (2 Sm 12:11). Similarly, the life-shortening ravages of AIDS may continue even though a person has repented of the sinful homosexual acts that may have caused it. Venereal disease from prostitution, the hardship of child-support incurred because of adultery or fornication—sin's painful consequences may be experienced for years after the sinner repents of those illicit relationships.

2. *Pray that God will use any person, even wayward companions or associates of your loved ones, as instruments to bring them back to the Lord.* Not just hurtful situations but also individuals of any moral character whatsoever can be used by God to bring about someone's conversion. Probably Jonah was the only person on board the ship who knew the true Lord, for at the height of the storm, "each cried out to his own god" (Jon 1:5). But the Lord used these pagans to alert Jonah to what was happening.

Likewise, runaway teenagers may learn only from those who

rape and rob them that street life is unsavory; attacks by such persons can bring them to realize that they will find security only in turning away from that sin-infested environment.

God can use anyone, good or bad, witting or unwitting, to nudge the sinner back to his merciful embrace. He can instrument conversion through repulsion for an exploitative pimp. He can work though the gentle compassion of a street-ministering "good Samaritan." A TV evangelist or the televised testimony of a sinner who found the Lord can be a catalyst for conversion. So commit your loved ones to God and ask him to bring them to a true and lasting conversion through the instruments of his choice.

3. *Pray that God will work in his way, not in a way that you choose, to dissolve the spiritual rebellion of the lapsed person.* Some who pray for their fallen-away loved ones try to contrive the *means* to restore them. They often fail because what is needed is not their way but God's way. "'My thoughts are not your thoughts, neither are your ways my ways,' declares the Lord" (Is 55:8). We see the situation narrowly, as if through a microscope, while God sees it broadly through a telescope. No way could anyone have known that God would provide "a great fish to swallow Jonah," or that he would suddenly calm the sea when Jonah was thrown overboard, or that the sailors would be impacted by the miracle and be converted to reverence the true Lord and make sacrifices to him (see Jonah 1:15-17). Who would have guessed that Jonah's turning back to the Lord would itself become an evangelistic event resulting in the conversion of others?

God may be using events in the lives of your fallen-away loved ones in many unseen ways, especially if you pray for that without demanding evidence of it. Initially, once you have begun interceding, it may even seem that things are getting worse. But this may indicate that God is applying more pressure to soften hardened hearts—as well as to test your own faith to the very limit. Remember: it was only after three days in the stomach of the great fish that Jonah finally promised to obey God's call. If the rebellion of your relatives seems to be similarly unrelenting, still you must persist in praying for their supernatural protection during the time of prolonged resistance.

Just knowing that you cannot choose conversion for someone else can relieve you of much pressure. Even God himself will not force anyone to repent against his or her will. In his mysterious providence, however, your prayers can elicit from God the outpouring of powerful "graces of persuasion" on your loved ones.

4. *Ask God that your fallen-away loved ones will bring about his glory by their personal holiness and evangelizing influence after their conversion.* Sometimes the greatest holiness and most fruitful ministry of a person's life comes after the deepest repentance. The mighty ministry for which Jonah is remembered occurred after he abandoned his futile attempt to ignore God's call. If Mary Magdalen hadn't been a sinner, she probably never would have rebounded with such tender love for Jesus and probably never would have become a saint. The most powerful testimonies come from repentant sinners. Certainly "there will be more rejoicing in heaven over one sinner who repents than over ninety-nine righteous persons who do not need to repent" (Lk 15:7).

Jonah's post-conversion preaching brought about an astonishing revival of prayer and penance in Nineveh, one of the largest cities of the world at that time. By divine ingenuity, God worked through Jonah's wrong choices to lead him to the center of the divine will and purpose. He came to know God's patience and mercy, and he proved that a sinner can be used by God in powerful ways. Jonah's story bespeaks a message of hope for dejected sinners—and also for those who watch, wait, and pray for them.

The great St. Paul became history's greatest missionary after his conversion from practicing terrorism against Christians, converting countless souls even today by his epistles. Peter too needed some converting after disgracing his papal office by denying Christ three times; he found that Christ himself was his intercessor and that he was being invited to intercede for his companions: "I have prayed for you, Simon, that your faith may not fail. And when you have turned back, strengthen your brothers" (Lk 22:32). A weak person who is converted is often given strength by God to convert others in a sort of ripple effect. This afterglow should be one of the prayer intentions of those who plead for the return of their loved ones.

5. *Pray that the conversion of your loved ones will be deep, definite, and permanent.* After his great conversion, Jonah slipped back into rebellion against God: he was angry because God relented from his threatened punishment of Nineveh when its people repented of their sins (see Jonah 4:1-3). Perhaps Jonah was embarrassed because he felt that God had made him look like a false prophet. Whatever the reason, God had to patiently guide Jonah back from rebellion. Many souls are like that. Like a compass needle that keeps fluctuating after a disturbing magnetic influence has been removed, some people keep wavering, requiring sometimes many days or weeks to become steady in keeping their efforts God-directed. This is a time for intercessors to persevere in follow-up prayer for these returning prodigals.

Like the Good Shepherd who not only picks up the lost sheep from the briar patch but also carries it in his arms and holds it close, those who are prayer-shepherds must not be satisfied with disengaging a soul from the thornbush of sin by their prayers. They must "carry" that soul in warm support and fellowship, as a defense against Satan, who will try every stratagem to recapture his former serf.

In the early Church, pastoral care and concern for such neophyte converts, called catechumens, was given top priority. The story is told that St. John the Evangelist once left one of his converts in the pastoral care of a bishop at Ephesus. This bishop was neglectful of his duty to provide support, encouragement, and prayer for the catechumen, and so the catechumen apostatized from the Church. It is reported that St. John rebuked the bishop with the words:

> Alas, Alas! To what a guardian have I entrusted our brother! The Church is a family, and we are our brother's keeper, both for those entering it and those returning to it. These babes in Christ are not to be left to starve or chill or die under neglect. They leave their old companions in sin, and we must help them find others in the Church to take their place in holy companionship. Before the Judge on reckoning day, we should be able to say, "Here am I and the children thou hast given me. Not one of them is lost."[1]

Centuries have passed but this is still good advice for today, when the Church's hemorrhaging of souls is more pronounced than ever before.

In all your prayers for your fallen-away loved ones, cling tenaciously to God's promises: "You, O God, tested us; you refined us like silver... We went through fire and water, but you brought us to a place of abundance" (Ps 66:10-12). That abundance is granted to faithful intercessors who anguish over their faith-weak loved ones. We see it demonstrated in the case of Job: *"After he had prayed for his friends,* the Lord made him prosperous again and gave him twice as much as he had before" (Jb 42:10).

Intercessors who are faithful to their privileged calling to release God's boundless mercy soon come to recognize that the God they are praying to is the God of the hundredfold, abounding in mercy.

TWENTY-ONE

Boosting Your Love Potential

The pastor of a mountain church in the Ozarks called his staff together to vote on whether to buy a much-needed chandelier for the church. One hillbilly deacon objected. "First off, nobody here knows how to spell chandelier; second, nobody knows how to play it; and third, what we really need is more light."

Not all suggested improvements are appreciated by the beneficiaries, even when those beneficiaries are ourselves. As some punster put it, we all have a chance to improve, but some people don't take chances. Yet we are all in the biggest room in the world—the room for improvement. Filtering through the gospel truths is an underlying Christian improvement dynamic sometimes called the *"principle of the extra measure."* This is a mandate inherent in Christianity that urges us to aspire vigorously and relentlessly to maximum spiritual growth. It is a norm that urges us to keep our gears operating in overdrive. It is a challenge that is epitomized in Jesus' challenge to be, not mediocre, but "perfect as your heavenly Father is perfect" (Mt 5:48).

The basement level of the spiritual skyscraper is the "be ye evil" level. On the fiftieth floor is the "be ye good" department, while the "be ye perfect" department is on the 100th floor. The intermediate floors, of course, are graded to variant levels of virtue. Many ignore the Augustinian warning sign posted by the elevator buttons: "When thou are satisfied with thyself, thou art lost!"—so they get off at the fiftieth floor, where the Smugness Company, Inc. has its offices. They never make it up to the 100th floor where Jesus presides as Chief Executive Officer in the "be ye perfect" department, where the company slogan is: "God loves us as we are, but he loves us too much to leave us this way."

WHAT ARE YOU GOOD FOR?

I always get a chuckle out of the oft-quoted rib-tickler about the young lad who boasted to his friend that his Daddy was a doctor, so he could be "sick for nothing." Not to be upstaged, the other lad retorted, "So what? My Daddy's a minister, so I can be good for nothing."

To be virtuous, one has to be "good for something." If God labelled each of us with mathematical symbols, the "good for nothing" would be marked with a minus sign, the "good" with an equal sign (connoting spiritual neutrality), and the "good for somethings" with a plus sign.

Very few Christians are total minuses—so sinful that their evil desires eclipse their good ones. But how many of us might reasonably expect to be marked with a plus? It is not that we maliciously seek evil as such; we simply choose to do what we want to do rather than what we ought to do. Our usual preference is simply to follow the path of least resistance. But, as one quipster remarked, seeking the least resistance is what makes rivers and men crooked.

Jesus tells us to aim higher—to keep shooting for the stars even if we only keep hitting the treetops. But the greatest failing for most of us is not that our target is too high and we miss it, but that our target is too low and we hit it. "Let your light shine before men, that they may see your good deeds," Jesus tells his hearers (Mt 5:16) after challenging them with his discourse on the Beatitudes (which must have nonplused them with its paradoxes on happiness in mourning, and the like). Note that only good deeds can shine out as light; the mere absence of bad deeds carries no evangelistic impact. In effect, Jesus implicitly affirmed the truth of the old bromide that "Nobody ever does his best; that's why we can all do better."

Jesus calls us to reach beyond the negative righteousness of simply refraining from sin—being good by not being bad. That would be to stop on the fiftieth floor of the spiritual skyscraper. On this subject he minces no words: "I tell you, unless your *righteousness* surpasses that of the Pharisees and teachers of the law, *you will certainly not enter the kingdom of heaven*" (Mt 5:20). Jesus thus taught that the very acts of righteousness can be nonrighteous; they "will have no reward" if they are motivated by the wrong inner dispositions—for instance, if they are performed to be noticed by others (Mt 6:1).

The scribes and Pharisees strove to obey the "thou shalts" and the "thou shalt nots"—and it is true that Jesus affirmed the need to fulfill such laws faithfully (see Matthew 5:19). Yet he also added an "extra measure" to the Law of Moses by refining it, for he came "not to abolish the Law but to fulfill it" by giving it its fullest meaning (Mt 5:17). Jesus emphasized the deep principles underlying the Law and stressed the need for an extra measure of *internalized* commitment to it, *over and above* the mere external acknowledgment and obedience that were practiced by the scribes and Pharisees.

THAT MAGNANIMOUS "EXTRA MEASURE"

It is especially in chapter five of Matthew's Gospel that we see Jesus presenting this principle through examples of contrast. Not that he polarizes his teachings over against the Old

Testament (on the contrary, he has just established the validity of the Law in that same chapter). Rather, Jesus fleshes out the rabbinic tradition's interpretation of the Law, which had tended to focus on external observance.

Jesus considered this principle of extra measure to be of such paramount importance that he sought to highlight it with a series of six counterpoints: "You have heard thus and so... but I tell you that..." In chapters six and seven he offers another dozen examples of practices to be polished with the extra measure of heroic virtue. It is in this setting that Jesus says it is not enough to avoid murder, but that even anger is to be controlled; not enough to avoid adultery, but even unchaste thoughts; not enough to fulfill legal requirements for divorce, but to avoid it altogether (except for unfaithfulness); not enough to fulfill an oath, but to avoid taking any oath lightly; not enough to claim just retribution when defrauded, but to turn the other cheek and forego retaliation; not enough to love your friends, but also your enemies. Further extra measure norms prescribed by Jesus include fasting and being generous and prayerful, but not conspicuously; having normal concern, but never worry or anxiety; acknowledging our own guilt, but not rashly judging others concerning theirs.

In his parable Jesus excoriated the self-righteousness of the Pharisee who boasted in prayerful gratitude, "God, I thank you that I am not like other men—robbers, evildoers, adulterers—or even like this tax collector" (Lk 18:11). Jesus was quick to affirm that the righteousness of legality was above savagery, but far below magnanimity. The true Christian asks not, "How little can I get by with, without sinning?"—like the faithful Sunday churchgoer who cultivates no private prayer life. Rather, the true Christian asks, "In this situation, how great are the possibilities for my growing spiritually and glorifying God?"

Most of us respond to an extra measure of insult with an extra measure of indignation. But this is not the extra measure to which Jesus calls us! As a simple test of which type of extra measure you lean toward, ask yourself how you respond to being insulted, reviled, or persecuted. Is your reaction one of: a) resentment; b) tolerance; or c) rejoicing with the extra measure of "exceeding gladness," because of the extra measure of your reward in heaven (see Matthew 5:11)? Is your forgiveness extended: a) zero times; b) seven times; or c) "seventy times seven times" (symbolizing the extra measure of limitless forgiveness that Jesus requires)?

One obstacle to our seeking to live according to Jesus' extra measure is the "I'm good enough" mentality that pervades our society. Witness the husband who is not a wife-beater, but not much of a wife-hugger either. Or the wife who is not a husband-nagger, but not much of a husband-complimenter either. Or the parent who doesn't belittle the child, but doesn't often encourage or affirm the child. Include in this list the person who doesn't criticize others, but seldom praises them. And the one who never gossips about others, but doesn't defend them either when they are victims of slander. There are those who never refuse a request for a favor, yet never spontaneously offer help. There are many who would never think of stealing, but neither would they generously donate to the needy. Others may refrain from prosecuting a purse-snatcher, but not offer financial assistance for rehabilitation. The element of heroism in virtue is at a premium in our society and does not flourish today as it did among the Christians of apostolic times.

ALL YOU NEED IS LOVE—HEROIC LOVE

Any virtue can be said to be heroic to the extent that it is supercharged with love. "Over *all these virtues* put on love, which binds them all together in perfect unity" (Col 3:14). This is why Jesus discusses—and spotlights—the principle of the extra measure in his teaching about the virtue of charity.

It required heroic love to go beyond obeying the legal demands of the occupying Roman soldiers who could require a Jew to carry their military gear: "If someone forces you to go one mile, go with him two miles" (Mt 5:40-41). Heroic love was to be the normative response to being offended by others: "To the one who would take your tunic, give him your cloak as well…. Pray for those who persecute you…. If you love only those who love you, what reward will you get?… If you greet only your brothers, *what are you doing more than others? Do not even pagans do that?"* (Mt 5:40-47). Jesus' words are clearly an invitation—and a mandate—to boost our love potential beyond mediocrity.

On those rare occasions when this extra measure of love is practiced in our day, it does not fail to edify. Some Communist rebels in a Korean town murdered a young Christian man who was a YMCA secretary (as Proverbs 29:10 warns us: "Bloodthirsty men seek to kill the upright"). At the trial, the slain boy's father, a minister, asked the judge to spare the life of the rebels' young leader. Moreover, he asked permission to adopt this cutthroat as his son to replace the son who had been murdered. As a result of this extra measure of forgiving love, the young Communist and all his relatives were converted to Christianity.

What is the source of such heroic love? The answer is found in the very command to love with the extra measure, in the words *"I* say to you…" (Mt 5:44). The secret of love and its glacier-melting warmth can be found only in the person of Jesus. He did not say, "Without my ideals, you can do nothing," or "Without my precepts, you can do nothing." Jesus said, "Without *me* you can do nothing." Impossible to live the Sermon on the Mount unless the Savior of the Mount lives in you. "And this is how we know that he lives in us," says John. "We know it by the Spirit he gave us" (1 Jn 3:24).

Giving the extra measure of love is not always easy, but Jesus' demand is uncompromising: "I tell you… love your enemies, do good to those who hate you, bless those who curse you, pray for those who mistreat you…. If anyone takes what belongs to you, do not demand it back…. Love your enemies, do good to them, lend to them without expecting to get anything back.

Then your reward will be great" (Lk 6:27-35). When your enemy reaches for your head to smash it, you must reach for his heart to melt it. Great love—the extra measure—will bring an extra measure of a great reward: "A good measure, pressed down, shaken together and running over, will be poured into your lap. For with the measure you use, it will be measured to you" (Lk 6:38).

GOING THE EXTRA MILE

Jesus sheds light on the principle of the extra measure by the positive formulation he gives to the so-called Golden Rule: "In everything, do to others what you would have them do to you, for this sums up the Law and the Prophets" (Mt 7:12; Lk 6:31). In rabbinic Judaism, Hinduism, Buddhism, and Confucianism, this concept is expressed more negatively: "Do *not* unto others what you would *not* have them do to you." A little reflection will reveal that this positive demand is more far-reaching than the negative. Whereas the latter simply requires that we refrain from hurting others, the former requires that we also do good to them, compliment, affirm, encourage, and support them— just as we would like others to do to us.

In Christ's eyes the glory of the Good Samaritan of his parable was his application of the extra measure principle. Out of compassion, the rescuer saved the life of a Jew, knowing that Jews generally despised Samaritans. And not only that: he also left extra money for the innkeeper to care for the victim and promised even more money later if necessary. The bounty of his spirit overflowed the narrow boundaries of race and nationality, of class and traditional prejudice.

All four Gospels mention the woman—traditionally identified as Mary Magdalen—who exercised the extra measure of love by anointing Jesus with a most expensive perfume, even breaking the precious alabaster container to expend its total contents on her beloved. Judas and the other shriveled souls who objected could not understand love's reckless generosity.

Christ's extra measure principle stands enshrined in such stories and parables in the pages of God's Word. Our task is to enshrine it in our hearts: "Let the word of Christ dwell in you richly," says Paul (Col 3:16). Love must not be merely rhapsodized; it must be lived. Hence, Paul urges the Ephesians, "Be very careful how you live, making the *most* of every opportunity" (Eph 5:17).

Imagine a rifle marksman with excellent aim who never pulls the trigger, or a skilled bowman who never releases the arrow. Admiring the Christian ideal without practicing it is like aiming but never shooting. But for most of us, this ideal of the extra measure remains just an ideal, never becoming a reality. Perhaps that is why Jesus closed his treatise on the extra measure on a downbeat: "Small is the gate and narrow the road that leads to life, and only a few find it" (Mt 7:14).

Reading Paul's classic description of love, with its fifteen characteristics (see 1 Corinthians 13:4-7), we might well feel that the ideal is beyond our reach. And it is—unless we learn to practice the extra measure of love—a love which, Paul says, "always protects, trusts, hopes and perseveres." However faltering our attempts, we must plunge in with God's help and really aim to practice this ideal in our daily life. Pie in the sky will not do, for as Jesus warns, "Everyone who hears these words of mine and *does not put them into practice* is like a foolish man who built his house on sand" (Mt 7:26).

And to those with the "I'm good enough" mentality, the Lord also has a warning—the one given to the Church in Sardis: "Wake up! Strengthen what remains and is about to die, for I have not found your deeds complete in the sight of my God" (Rv 3:2). Or perhaps he is calling through the warning and lament he gave to the Church in Laodicea: "I know your deeds, that you are neither cold nor hot. I wish you were either one or the other. So, because you are lukewarm, neither hot nor cold, I am about to spit you out of my mouth" (3:15-16).

To restate our earlier question, if the Lord were to label you now, would it be with a minus sign, an equal sign, or a plus sign? Only authentic Christians would be marked with the plus sign—that is, the sign of the cross, the sign of the "plus" or "extra" measure.

This sign has two parts: the upright stroke depicting the vertical beam of the cross, called the *stipes;* and the horizontal stroke depicting the crossbeam, called the *patibulum*. The vertical represents the first precept of love—love for God—that demands an extra measure in order to "love him with our whole heart, soul, mind and strength." The horizontal represents the second precept of love—love for our neighbor and ourself—which also demands an extra measure to recognize and love Christ in even "the least of his brethren." Together, the two parts of the cross symbolize the greatest measure of love: "greater love than this no man has"—Jesus' own sacrificial love.

When, by our grace-response, we have boosted our love potential to consistently reflect Christlike love interiorly and exteriorly, then we can know that we are full-fledged Christians. Then we will have mastered the greatest challenge of Christianity, which is also its very hallmark—that of love's extra measure.

EPILOGUE

The Five "A's"

The question has been posed many times and in many ways, but it is still intriguing: If it were illegal to be a Christian, would your life provide enough evidence for your arrest?

Living as Christ lived is the validating feature of anyone who calls himself or herself a Christian. And something about this should be observable to others. Acts 11:26 says that the pagans in Antioch began to call Christ's followers "Christians"—not just "followers of the Way," as they had been known previously. Those pagans must have recognized *Christlike features* in the lives of those following Jesus' teachings.

Certainly, it is to be hoped that in a time of anti-Christian persecution our behavior would provide enough evidence for arrest! (By the way, Jesus warned that persecution will be widespread in the coming end times; see Luke 21:22-24). But even in the absence of persecution, we face the challenge of giving proof that we are imitating Jesus in our daily lives.

But precisely what constitutes this Christlike behavior, and what makes it observable by others? A close survey of God's Word reveals that there are five general areas where Christlike living comes to the surface. I call these the five "A" areas: Attitudes, Actions, Affections, Associations, and Ambitions. I have touched on all of these in this book; in fact, "the five A's" is one way to summarize its message.

1. *Attitudes.* Thoughts and feelings invariably emerge in actions and behavior (for instance, in body language, the study of which

has become a sophisticated science). In many ways, we are what we think, and ultimately this cannot be concealed (see Proverbs 26:24-26).

It is true that "if anyone is in Christ, he is a new creation" (2 Cor 5:17). But Paul warns us that this new state requires maintenance: "Do not conform any longer to the pattern of this world, but be transformed by the *renewing of your mind*" (Rom 12:2). Using Christ-engendered courage and strength (see Philippians 4:13), the true Christian's attitude is secure in its confident trust in the Lord. The Christian is aware that "through faith he is shielded by God's power" (1 Pt 1:5) and can therefore easily dispel anxiety: "Cast all your anxiety on him, for he cares for you" (1 Pt 5:7).

That attitude of security carries over into encounters with the enemy, "because the one who is within you is greater than the one who is in the world" (1 Jn 4:4). In general, the mindset of a true Christian is secure, tranquil, confident, and above all incandescent with love for God and other people.

2. *Actions.* Actions do speak louder than words. Our actions—and reactions as well—especially in hurtful situations reveal the depth of our relationship with God. When Job had lost his wealth, health, and even his children, he could cry out, "Though he slay me, yet will I hope in him" (Jb 13:15).

Paul was whipped, stoned, imprisoned, shipwrecked, and nearly starved, while his triple prayer plea against the "thorn in the flesh" was left apparently unanswered; the Spirit warned him of even more imprisonment and hardships, and yet he was unmoved by all such afflictions (see Acts 20:24). His apostolic action was like driving a bulldozer through a mine field. He averred that "everyone who wants to live a godly life in Christ Jesus will be persecuted," and he told Timothy to continue in what he had learned (see 2 Timothy 3:12, 14). He was intransigently convinced that "in all things God works for the good of those who love him" (Rom 8:28)—which was perhaps his own rephrasing of Proverbs 16:4: "The Lord works out everything for his own ends." In Paul we see that the actions of a true Christian, which express personal love for God, are always favorably productive, abounding in the fruit of the Spirit (see Galatians 5:22-23).

3. Affections. Christian affection is full-fledged *agape* love involving the heart, soul, and mind (see Matthew 22:37). The Christian seeks first the kingdom of God (see Matthew 6:33), and love for God in Christ is the driving force that integrates all other loves—for family, friends, and even reasonable material needs. This God-fused love is hard to describe but is easily recognized by others—"evidence" that one is truly Christian.

4. Associations. "Friendship with the world [worldly people with immoral values] is hatred toward God," James pronounces (Jas 4:4). Paul urges us to "purify ourselves from everything that contaminates body and spirit, perfecting holiness out of reverence for God" (2 Cor 7:1). If we are not with the Lord we are against him, Jesus warns (see Matthew 12:30).

While we may associate with sinners, as Jesus did, to attract them to God (without jeopardizing our own spiritual welfare), but our major associations should be with fellow-believers: "Do two walk together unless they have agreed?" (Am 3:3). Poor choices in this area can have serious consequences. Samson chose the wrong type of friends and lost his strength, eyes, and freedom. Demas' associations with world-lovers caused him to go astray and abandon Paul (see 2 Timothy 4:10).

Warm and loving friendship with God's blessed angels and with his inspiring and heroic saints is a privilege beyond compare. "Surrounded by such a great cloud of witnesses" (Heb 12:1) who encourage us on our Godward trek to heaven, a Christian shows evidence of being uplifted and enriched by their example, rejoicing that with them we all belong to "God's whole family in heaven and on earth" (Eph 3:15).

5. *Ambitions.* Wrong ambitions can pull us toward the infernal abyss—like ambition for money, for *"love* of money is the root of all kinds of evil" (1 Tm 6:10). But ambition for "treasures in heaven" pulls us heavenward (see Matthew 6:19-21). A Christian knows that what he "deposits in heaven" will not be stolen or deteriorate in value.

Show me a person with Paul's ambitions and I'll show you evidence for a champion Christian. His ambitions are absurdities to a worldling: "I want to know Christ and the power of his resurrection and the fellowship of sharing his sufferings, becoming like him in his death" (Phil 3:10). Job's ambition was to "go to his [God's] dwelling" (Jb 23:3). The psalmist waxes glowingly lyrical in expressing his ambition: "As the deer pants for streams of water, so my soul pants for you, O God. My soul thirsts for God.... when can I go and meet with God?" (Ps 42:1-2).

The hallmarks of a true follower of Christ in this life, comprise evidence that is never complete, for we are still *in statu viae*—still on pilgrimage. But when we are *in statu termini,* in the awesome presence of our Creator, and he draws us into his eternal embrace, evidence will no longer be relevant. Our goal will have been attained. It will mark the end of the beginning, and the beginning of the endless—a homecoming with bliss eternal, a joy beyond description!

Notes

FOUR
Treatment for Anemic Christians

1. "Constitution on the Sacred Liturgy," Article 7.

FIVE
Obeying God's Will—Gateway to Security

1. James Leen, *By Jacob's Well* (New York: P.J. Kenedy & Sons, 1940).

SEVEN
Amazing Grace—
Your Expandable Quota of Divine Life

1. C.S. Lewis, *Mere Christianity* (New York: Macmillan, 1952).

EIGHT
Miracle Power at Your Fingertips

1. John Flavel, *The Mystery of Providence* (Carlisle, Pa.: Banner of Truth, 1976).
2. Quoted in "News at a Glance," *Pentecostal Evangel,* April 1993, 15.

NINE
Mary, "Our Tainted Nature's Solitary Boast"

1. *Lumen gentium,* art. 51.
2. For proof of that doctrine, see my book, *Mary in the Bible* (Huntington, Ind.: Our Sunday Visitor, 1993).
3. *Lumen gentium,* art. 62.

TWELVE
The Art of Suffering—Way to Grow

1. From prayer card, "Your Cross," published by Claretian Tape Ministry, P.O. Box 19100, Los Angeles, CA 90019.

FOURTEEN
Coping with Life's Darkest Moments

1. C.S. Lewis, *A Grief Observed* (New York: Bantam, 1976).

SIXTEEN
Nestling in the Hand of God

1. *"Dei Filius,"* #1.

TWENTY
When Loved Ones Turn from God

1. As quoted in Elon Foster, ed., *6000 Sermon Illustrations* (Grand Rapids, Mich.: Baker, 1992), 138.

Editors Note: Every effort has been made to locate the original source of citations in this book. The publisher would welcome the opportunity to correct any omissions at the first opportunity.